DI-VER

Volume III

By Mike Bicks & Others

A Further Collection of Poems

And Their Raison d'Etre

Illustrated by Frank Webb

Frank

1992

Published in Porthmadog, Gwynedd, North Wales, by
Madoc Consultants

Other Books by Mike Bicks

DIV - VERS - ION Volume I   1988

DIV - VERS - ION Volume II 1990

Copyright © 1992 Mike Bicks, Penrhyndeudraeth, Gwynedd   0766 771360
Copyright © 1992 Frank Webb, Earlswood, Warwickshire   056 46 3576

British Library Cataloguing-in-Publication Data
A catalogue record for this book is available from the British Library

ISBN 1 897838 03 4

First Published November 1992 by

Madoc Consultants

65 Madoc Street West, Porthmadog, Gwynedd, LL49 9DU
0766 512237

Distribution Address

1 High Street, Penrhyndeudreath, Gwynedd, LL48 6BN
0766 771360

Design and Typography

Glen Cargill, BSc, MIEE, Chartered Engineer, Madoc Consultants

Body Typeface- CG Times 8pt

Printed in UK by West Tower Press Ltd   0533 313424

DI - VERS - ION III

DID YOU KNOW THAT

'NAUTICAL' IS AN ANAGRAM OF 'A LUNATIC'?

APPROPRIATE, DON'T YOU THINK!

CONTENTS

Title	Author	Page
Ode to a Special Person	Ron Bailey	6
A Soldier's Thoughts		9
Only Joking		10
Diolch yn Fawr		11
Porthmadog (Rap)		11
The Serene Years		13
Who's in Charge?		14
Our Mum, God Rest Her Soul		15
The Corgi Todds		16
After Dinner Speech		18
Mini-Saga - Fountain Pen		19
Medium Sized Saga - Big John		20
Big Frank		20
Put Down Moon, My 'Oppo' Said		22
The Sun Worshippers		24
The Black Rock Bad Guys		25
Dear Heather…	Linos E. Leat, Gnome	26
Harbour Dues	Mike Quinnell	28
Harbour Dues - My Reply		28
Extra Terrestrials		30
A Wedding Congratulation	Don Winterman	31
The Yellow Form	Don Winterman (Who Else)	32
Frank 'Shala' and the Speedboats	Don Winterman	32
My Friend	Stephen Townsend	37
After	Stephen Townsend	37
An Acknowledgement	G.E.Garley	37
A Ticking Off	Hilary Roberts	38
Why is a Boat Called 'She'		38
Bondo		40
A Boat Would be Good	Ilona Jones	40
Patience		41
David's Birthday Card		42
Christmas Gifts	Emma Grayson	43
Cats - Taff		44
Cats - Cunningham		44
Cats - Daisy		45
Cats - Lyn and Joan		46
Mrs Bouquet		46
The Weeping Willow	Alan Windsor	48
The Oak Tree	Alan Windsor	49
Red Indian Tragedy	Alan Windsor	51
Singapore - The Requirement		53

Singapore - Upon Independence		54
Sun-Light in Madog - A Sonnet to Slim		55
Sailing - for Pleasure?		55
Immortal Sails		56
A Christmas Carol		57
Sounds in the Garden	Emma Grayson	58
Join the Club	Anon. but supplied by Rosemary Gray	59
Three Bad Sailors	Gareth Hickman	59
My Get-up-and-Go	Kath Mackenzie	60
Airborne Warriors	Gareth Hickman	61
It's a 'B' Growing Old	Peggy Parmenter	63
Please, Mum, I Want my Ears Pierced	Emma Grayson	64
Is Death the Worst Option?		65
That Cold White Stuff	Gareth Hickman	66
Jenna	Gareth Hickman	66
Mummy, I've Got the 'Flu'	Gareth Hickman	67
The Anti Abortion Lobby		67
The Soft Voice of Unreason	Jacqui Thomson	68
The Milking Parlour	Jacqui Thomson	69
Pale Moon		70
A Mugging		71
Ode to Dad	Roberta Halling	72
How Old are You?		72
Faint Heart Never Won Fair Lady		74
Admission		75
Intellectual Intercourse		75
Sunset Girl		76
Enquiring into Life		77
Pulling it Down	Lyn Dawe	79
Micro	Justine Merry	80
The Glaslyn Horizon		81
The bit you've all been waiting for		81

COLOUR PLATES

Eric Mills	7
Porthmadog	12
Moon	23
Power Boats	35
Indian Tragedy	50
Navigator	62
Ballast Isle	73
Glaslyn Horizon	78

DEDICATION

When I first met Eric Mills I was an 'on-the-point-of-retiring' Naval Lieutenant and he was the Boat Yard Proprietor who employed me for my 'getting-used-to-being-a-civilian' month.   I'll never forget the look on his face when I asked, "Could you employ me.... but you mustn't pay me anything?" He called up to Peter his manager, "Hey! Christmas has come early this year!"

I liked Eric then, I've admired him in between, and now, some twenty one years later, I still think he is a great guy.

He, it was, who rebuilt my yacht when it was quite badly damaged, back in 1974. He saved me a considerable amount of money.

It is to Eric that I dedicate this book, to Eric and the high standards which he represents.

His wife, Mary, also deserves a mention... even though she's a Geordie. They do say that behind every successful man there is a woman...

"Ode to a Special Person"

Is there a problem with your boat or its machinery?
Looking for marvels of repair in wood or G.R.P.?
Or do you just want sound advice on matters of the sea?
Then go and have a chat with Good Old Eric!

His casual charm and careless garb are traits one must not chide
For Underneath his secret lies, a gift he cannot hide -
Perfection in his workmanship, success in all that's tried
By the man his neighbours know as "Good Old Eric".

He's seldom in his shed but, when you need him, never mind;
If you listen for the whistling he won't be far behind.
Working away, quite merrily, on boats is where you'll find,
The quality and style of Good Old Eric.

Eric was born, most probably, three hundred years too late;
He would have been notorious, an infamous pirate;
Instead the world, in self denial, had all those years to wait
For the man known to his friends as Good Old Eric.

Opposite - **A Special Person- Eric Mills**

DOWN TO BUSINESS

I commenced the draft of this book at a time when the world was, yet again, off balance due to the inhumanity of one of its inhabitants.

It hardly seemed appropriate to be frivolous when brave young men and women were putting their lives at risk for the sake of what we believe to be 'Justice': and, though I love it, I have always thought 'poetry' to be synonymous with frivolity.

But then came flooding into my mind all the arguments against that attitude. Indeed, is it not so that poems often result from emotional or even traumatic situations.

Quite often one hears a lyrical interpretation of the most bizarre circumstances - "And there shall be in that rich earth...." for example.

So I pressed on, helped and encouraged by many people. Life must go on, in spite of Sad Damned Hinsane and his Mob. He is not the first nor, dare I say, will he be the last to upset the apple-cart.

Back in 1950, two young brothers were serving the aims of Justice in Malaya. Anyone who has been involved with jungle warfare will understand the particular terror that it can generate; a terror enhanced in their situation by an uncertainty as to who, precisely, was friend and who foe.

One of the boys wrote a poem in June 1950. A copy of it has been sent to me by my friend, Stephen Townsend, (who, incidentally, writes the most comprehensive Transport Guides) on behalf of the writer's mother who is now in her eighties. The boy himself, sadly, died shortly after his return home. He had contracted Hodgkinson's disease.

In his covering letter stephen said, "I don't know if this is good poetry. I don't really understand what makes good or bad poetry. I would have thought it is a matter of personal taste."

I have to agree with him; but I would add, possibly in my own defence, that there are times when not only should the words be taken into account but also the environment in which they were written. In this case steamy, primary jungle with who-knows-what hidden behind the next tree.

Can one wonder at:-

"A Soldier's Thoughts."

When on these foreign shores I tread,
Them Bandits I do really dread;
Underneath a blazing sun,
Fighting them is not much fun.

Armoured only with a gun,
Very soon I'll make them run,
When the bullets start to fly,
"Get them!" will be my battle-cry.

Soon the jungle will be clear,
When the end is very near.
Perhaps, then, we will get some rest
And I can say, "I've done my best!".

Then across the silver foam,
On a ship I'll come sailing home.
Never more I'll want to roam,
And with this line I'll end this poem.

Stephen told me, "When I explained to Ron's mother your intention to include his poem in your book, she was over the Moon. It was quite touching for her, I think, as you may expect. I suppose it is nice for her to think that a little of 'Lost son' will live on, somewhere."

That is reason enough for me. To have pleased someone is to have achieved something worthwhile.

Stephen and I fell into lengthy discussions on the relative merits of 'traditional' and 'modern' art forms, some of which you will see, later, if you read on. He also submitted a couple of his own attempts at poetry, 'for my use, if I want them'.

But first, let me tell you about Melia and Leanne.

These were a couple of youngsters who stayed with us on a Youth exchange visit in December, 1989. Melia was from Warragul, Victoria, and Leanne from Christchurch, New Zealand. They proved to be lively, almost cheeky, conversationalists, with a good sense of humour, so I decided to confront them with a challenge. Boy! Did they respond!

For the purposes of 'scan', and all that rubbish, I have to tell you that the Australian girl's name is pronounced with the accent on the 'i'.... Mel i̲ a.

I wrote:-

"Only Joking!"

I Hope God will forgive me if I say he made a blunder;
For Life, as we all know it, simply can't exist 'Down Under'.
Their Summer comes at Christmas time, their Winter in July;
The sun goes round the wrong way in their topsy-turvy sky.

I wonder; since they have a Queen, where does she wear her crown?
I'm told that every single thing, out there, is upside down.
So all that you and I do, in the comfort of our beds,
The Aussies and the Kiwis must do standing on their heads!

It must be so embarrassing - I don't know how they stick it -
For one lot can't play rugby.... and the others can't play cricket!

However nasty I might be, I really ought to say,
Two attri-beauts 'Down Under' has who'll make this Joker pay!
They brought a freshness to our lives. Thank God there is no ban
On Antipodean-s-exports like Melia and Leanne.

I gave them a copy each on the evening before their departure which, on reflection, was a bit cowardly, if not downright unfair, thinking that would be 'an end ont'! But not a bit of it! At breakfast, the following morning, Leanne, the argumentative one, handed me a folded piece of paper.

On it was their reply:-

"Diolch Yn Fawr"

Well, thank you, Mike, but as you can see
We're not as bad as you thought us to be.
We really are quite literate, compared to those....above,
And let me tell you, honestly, there's no problem making love!

We have a Queen and we're quite smart
To keep her and us miles apart.
We gave her to you and there is where she'll stay
To watch the Guards changing at eleven every day.

You know we can play rugby. We proved that just before;
And if you played 'Down Under' we'd kick you out the door!

Well, thank you, Mate. It's been just great
And this we've got to say;
That you and Joan and both the kids
Have been great in every way.

The note was signed- **Leanne Watkins and Melia Vickerman**.

When they were ready to leave, they handed us all sorts of gifts including 'T' shirts, badges and pennants, significant to their respective homes; and they have kept in touch. We had cards from them both, last Christmas.

It could be argued that I was let off lightly. It is also, though, supportive of my argument that we all have, lurking inside us, a would-be poet. Only snag is that some of us just can't seem to persuade him to come out into the open.

Over the Page - **Porthmadog**

WHY POETRY? Why the Rhyming Kind?

In 'Diversion 1', I asked the question, "Why poetry? And, what's more to the point, why the rhyming kind?"

Well I can answer that question more informatively perhaps, now than I could then. It is the challenge! It is the need, the determination to make a point, communicate a message, while still achieving a sense of rhythm and a degree of symmetry.

"Rap"... I think they call it... which must be one of the most recent forms of poetry to hit us, has taken the 'Pop' music scene by storm. It constitutes a challenge, if ever I saw one.

There was a competition announced in one of the Dailies, some time ago, offering prizes for 'Rap' style descriptions of competitor's home towns. I had a go but was never satisfied with the work. I let time lapse and then had a cast iron excuse for not sending it in... like I'd missed the deadline!

The resulting piece only gets into this book on the strength of cheek of the last rhyme, and to illuminate a point. It shows the lengths to which some people will go to achieve their ends!

"Porthmadog"

This town was built on heaps of silt
By people who were handy
With Mason's tools. They were no fools,
Although the ground was sandy.

The Main Street done, they had some fun
With side roads and back alleys;
But sad and plain was this terrain,
Between the hills and valleys.

Not far away, though, truth to say,
A short trek on a pony; a
Majestic place of charm and grace,
The mountains of Snowdonia.

* * * * * * * * * *

A cynic I may be; but what the Hell? Life is too short to be serious about everything.

The next item was written into a birthday card to be sent to a friend who, fast approaching sixty, thought the end was nigh. Those of you who have arrived, already, may understand the quite unnecessary trauma.

I regret the joke backfired a little bit on me, but I hope it cheered him up!

"The Serene Years"

When suddenly you realise how speedily have passed
The twenty years or so you thought would be your very last
And what you looked on as 'old age' seems now to be quite young;
Be proud, not sad! You've joined a group it's good to be among.

When travelling in crowded train, you're weary on your feet;
Be pleased that someone else must think to offer you his seat.
If worried by advancing years, be sated by this crumb:
The more advanced, the shorter a life sentence would become!

Life can be so cruel, sometimes! It wasn't long after writing those last couple of verses into the draft that my mother died.

She went in what I am told is the best possible way... She maintained her independence to the last, suffered a stroke and never regained consciousness. I hope it was painless for her and that she didn't know what was happening.

By Jove, she does now, if my beliefs are well founded.

I had reached that age whereat the professed atheist begins to have second thoughts, and even the uncommitted accepter starts to ask himself questions, like:-

"Who's in Charge?"

How much of what we do is by decision?
 How much of it is by the will of God?
The nature of the show
 Is such
That we may never know
 Until that final, upward path is trod!

How independent are our private feelings?
 Do Hope and Hate come naturally to Man?
When Joy or Envy rule
 Are they
Some Sacramental tool
 To help the execution of His plan?

It is difficult to credit that our actions
 Are guided by a tiny, inner voice;
When, often, we are told
 About a
Feat so mad, or bold,
 That our minds cannot accept it was by choice.

No!

The Voice must be external to the Ego.
 We must be guided by a power above.
The gamble is too great
 For Him
To leave to doubtful Fate
 The achievement of a Universal Love.

It was suggested by a member of the family that it would be 'nice' if I were to write an obituary to Mum, in verse.   -Trauma time!

I did my best. I felt, all the way through, that Mum was watching over my shoulder. I felt, strangely, like a schoolboy, over again and I remembered, so clearly, those far off days during the war when all I wanted to do was to watch the Spitfires taking off from Hornchurch Aerodrome but was made to sit in the kitchen and go over my spellings and 'times tables'. I'm sure I heard her say, "Get the grammar right, Boy! and no split infinitives!".

Between us we finished it. The rest of the family approved and I was invited to read the poem in the chapel at the Crematorium, down in Torbay, and then at the Remembrance and Interment ceremony at Treflys.

I argued with myself, long and hard, as to whether or not it should go into this book. To include it threatened to belittle my innermost thoughts and to denigrate the driving sentiment.

The other side won! This is my book! Mum had read as much of it as the Good Lord allowed. It is, after all, a personal record, shared only with those I truly love and/or respect.

Upon deep introspection, I believe she would be more annoyed if I left it out than critical of its inclusion.

"Our Mum, God Rest Her Soul."

There, in our early childhood, in those dark, drear days of war,
   Her philosophical approach, her ever open store
Of courage, sense and fortitude, her scorn for Evil's might
   Gave strength and reassurance 'gainst the perils of the night.

She typified the Spirit which a mother, surely, needs
   In steering errant kids away from silly, childish deeds.
Through all the different phases of our lives she has been there
   To praise, rebuke or censure with a moving, loving care.

As we've agreed, she made us work! She did so with a zest
   Which was, itself, encouragement: we had to do our best.
She taught us certain standards and, thereafter, made it clear,
   "You're never so big that I can't reach to clip you round the ear!"

In all of us who knew her, of course a sadness flows.
   The passing of a loved-one, and an era, I suppose,
Is bound to leave a scar across we mortals, left behind,
   When grief and pain; yes, even guilt, start gnawing at the mind.

So, Dan and Justine, everyone, I beg you, join with me
   In sending up this message, in contentment, if not glee.
"Now, Spirit, unencumbered by restrictive Earthly chains,
   We bid you, soar in freedom o'er those tranquil, Heavenly plains".

We thank you, Lord, for giving her the life on Earth she had
   And pray that you will help our Mum to find, and join, our Dad.

Dan, my brother, and Justine, my sister, both have mentions in previous Diversions. Dan was the naughty boy in Volume 1 who imitated the whistling bomb, and Justine actually contributed to Volume 2. She may get a line or two in here, if she behaves herself.

Mum was a great one for unfinished proverbs. "When in Rome....!" she used to say. Ah well, Mum, "When in heaven..."

Back to Earth; and to dwell for a few moments on the chance, or is it idiocy, which puts us, from time to time, into situations which, perhaps, we would have preferred to avoid.

I was advised , one day, that the top-mark was missing from No 3 buoy.

Now this is an extra special top-mark, partly because it is bigger than all the others, partly because I made it and mostly because the buoy marks the gap between North Bank and Harlech Spit.

I was annoyed!

Quick look at the watch- check the tide tables- I have time to go and see for myself.

I should have remembered that annoyance dulls the judgement... Didn't I fall off the wall because I was annoyed... and haven't I been known as Humpty Dumpty ever since!

This time I didn't check the weather.

To help you understand the next poem I should also explain that Bill and Joyce Todd were always known as "The Corgi Todds". This came about because when they applied for a mooring they asked, specifically, for a 'drying' berth so that their dog, a corgi, could go for a walk.

On the occasion about to be related they were out in their yacht, Lucida III, returning from Pwllheli, I think. They certainly appeared from the direction of Criccieth- and they had no right being out there at all!

"The Corgi Todds."

White knuckles gripping tiller for support,
I watched the bow come crashing down again
And wondered at this battle, often fought
Against all Reason! Am I so insane?

No Earthling with his 'marbles' safe in store
Would tempt the Elements so blatantly;
And on a vague suggestion, nothing more,
That all was 'not-quite-right' with No 3.

The wind, from South South West and in its stride,
was piling wave on wave upon the Bar.
Out there, you know, there is no place to hide
When Nature leaves her God-damned door ajar.

But there it was, the top-mark clearly gone
And no way dared I risk a closer scan;
So, waiting for a lull and thereupon
To turn; I felt a very lonely man.

Yet, what was that? The merest smudge of white!
A breaking wave?... It couldn't be a sail!
Perhaps a giant seagull's soaring flight.
I searched the turmoil but to no avail.

Wait! There it was again; much closer, now;
Atop a wave-crest, surfing, bold and free.
A sail, indeed! I knew... Don't ask me how!
It had to be the sloop Lucida Three.

A varnished clinker hull swept past my boat,
On starboard tack and going like a train.
It was, I swear, more airborne than afloat
And treating Madog's Cauldron with disdain.

Acknowledging the skipper's friendly wave,
I realized how cowardly I'd been;
For Bill and Joyce were, far from being brave,
Just lazing; a 'Neptunal' King and Queen.

I turned, then, feeling green around the gills,
To battle inwards, 'gainst enormous odds
And, even now, my recollection thrills
With admiration for those 'Corgi Todds'.

    Bill tells me he has just become eligible for a 'Bus pass', whatever that means...? He and Joyce put on a magnificent party with fantastic food and some memorable entertainment. I knew Bill was a choir-man... but I didn't know he could actually sing.
    The denouement of the story... Yes, the top-mark had been hacksawed off.
    Can you imagine the mentality of someone who would hacksaw the top from a navigation buoy? What for? A souvenir, perhaps! It takes all sorts...

... For instance; if you were the wife of the newly appointed Commodore of your Yacht Club, and you had to make an 'After-Dinner' speech at his inauguration, what would you say?

I made some hyperthetical suggestions as a 'fun' dig at a couple for whom, in reality, I have the greatest respect. Only with their permission would I even consider entering them into the book.

The bits in brackets are meant to be 'Stage whispers', uttered behind the back of the hand...

"After Dinner Speech"

"It's easy to be full of praise for him:
As yachtsmen come, he has to be the best.
(The rest are pretty dim).
I love to watch him navigate.
(It's running hard aground I hate:
That's when he puts my patience to the test).

It's magic when he lets me have a go.
'Just keep that smudge of smoke above the bow!'
He says, then goes below
And leaves me to the wind and spray.
The smudge of smoke blows clean away.
(I bet he thinks I'm such a silly cow!)

He must know what he's doing, don't you think!
(Though some say he's as thick as two short planks -
And takes too much to drink!)
If that were so; if he's a bore,
They wouldn't make him Commodore,
Would they! *(He'd be down amongst the ranks!)*

I jest, of course. He gets what he deserves:
A lovely fellow, no-one can deny,
With hardened, steel-like nerves.
He's done so much out in the wings
(And licked some boots, and pulled some strings) -
On stage he'll be an extra special guy."

No! I will not tell you who I had in mind! It would be totally wrong.

Come to think of it, though... I don't see why I should worry about 'permission'. I mean to say, she put rude things about me in her 'Madoc News' without asking permission!

Do you remember the craze that swept the world, not so long ago, for 'Mini Sagas'? There were competitions run by newspapers and magazines and even a published book of the damned things.

Why 'Damned'? Well, I had a go and failed, miserably. I knew it would never catch on as an 'Art Form'.

I had just found and fixed an old pen and was trying it out on a scrap of paper. I wrote:-

> *Once upon a time there was a Platignum fountain pen. Its nib was broken and it was very sad.*
>
> *Then a kindly old pen-lover found it lying, disused and unwanted, in a pen box. He cleaned it, repaired its nib, gave it a drink of the finest ink available and used it regularly.*
>
> *In return, the pen produced beautiful handwriting and prize winning Mini Sagas for its new master who, hitherto, had written only a load of rubbish.*
>
> *It just goes to show, doesn't it, that even a fountain pen can show gratitude. Aaaah!*

That's 95 words! 45 too many for it to qualify as a Mini Saga. How do they do it? It cannot be easy! Well, you try getting an introduction, a plot development and a climax into just fifty words!

In the above terms, what follows would possibly be called a medium sized saga. I expect you have heard the story... but it does lead me nicely into the next poem:-

The newly arrived bar tender at the saloon of a quaint little Western town could not understand why everyone was packing up and heading East, just because rumour had it that 'Big John' was coming to town. He stuck steadfastly to his post as the last covered wagon rolled along the Main Street. He scoffed at the Sheriff when that gentleman asked, "Are you sure you won't join me?", downed his whisky and strutted off.

A period of calm followed; an almost eerie silence. The bar tender began to feel lonely but consoled himself by a reminder that 'they' would all be back when they realised how stupid they were being!

Suddenly the ground shook: just a little tremor, at first, but closely followed by another... and another... each more violent than its predecessor. The glasses on the shelves rattled. A great shadow seemed to invade the entrance... and then... the swing-doors burst open: one came off its hinges.

The bartender saw the legs, waist and chest of a man framed in the doorway. Instantly it all became clear. He understood the urgent need to be somewhere else. His knees turned to liquid as the head and shoulders ducked into the saloon and this giant thundered over to the bar.

"Whisky!" rumbled a deep, reverberating bass, "And make it snappy! I haven't got long!"
"W w why's that?" stammered the bartender. "I th th thought you'd b b be st staying!"
"Good God, Man!" said the giant. "Haven't you heard? Big John's coming to town!"

In our case it was 'Big Frank'. He and his adorable family descended upon Porthmadog and instantly endeared themselves to everyone... OR ELSE!

One day, Mrs. V. de L. pointed to her husband who was leaning over the boom of his yacht and said to me, "Youm ought to write a poem about that!"

I could see what she meant. She was referring to the gap between the top of his trousers and the bottom of his 'T' shirt. I had to admit that, really speaking, for the sake of decorum, too much was revealed... so I wrote, anonymously...

"Big Frank"

Vast rolling hills where Nature's hand has been
Conceal in mystery the vale between;
And promise mountains more,
  Although,
Seen through this open door,
  The landscape I describe is PINK, not green!

The line of decency, when bends the chap,
Is guilty of infringement, as the gap
Displayed without repent,
  Is like
Some human continent:
  To find your way around you'd need a map!

> Yet, possibly, the 'bare' facts live a lie.
> This chauvinistic shell is just to try
> A devil-may-care plan
> To hide
> The softness of a man
> Who, truthfully, would never hurt a fly.
>
> If I've annoyed Big Frank I'm for the 'chop'!
> I surely hope he knows just when to stop!
> I think there'll be a war
> Though I
> Suspect the cannon's roar
> Is really a pea-shooter going POP!

Let's change the subject... Quick!

In the Royal Navy there existed a system whereby the 'Ordinary' Matelot could let the Drafting Office know where he would prefer to serve. It was called the 'Preference Drafting System' and it never worked.

An 845 Squadron colleague of mine once drew a superb cartoon to illustrate the shortcomings in the system. What follows, therefore, is only my interpretation of his idea.

As of old, some of you may need an explanation of some of the words and phrases:-

'Oppo'... An especial friend, quoting from 'Jackspeak'. It is derived from 'Opposite Number', the person who takes over one's station when one is 'off watch'.

'Ark'... of course, refers to H.M.S. Ark Royal.

'Crabs'... with due respect to Geoff Newbery, are those chaps who wear light blue, walk sideways and fly their aeroplanes only if all else fails.

'Tot'... specifically of 'Pusser's Rum'

'Aggie Weston's... Again I quote from 'Jackspeak'. The network of Royal Sailor's Rests begun in 1876 by the formidable Dame Agnes Weston. These Homes from Home still exist and flourish in Portsmouth, Gosport, Rosyth, Devonport and Plymouth. Their emphasis remains on home comforts-and temperance.

Such was Jack's genuine affection for his Sailor's Friend that when the warship H.M.S. Weston-Super-Mare was launched, she was immediately labelled 'Aggie-on-Horseback'!

There used to be one in Porthmadog, you know. I had the privilege, recently, of meeting the lady who, as a young girl, helped her mother to run it... Netta Day.

"Put Down 'Moon' My 'Oppo' Said"

"Put down 'Moon'", my 'Oppo' said, "Just for a flippin' lark.
Whatever you put you know you'll end up in the flippin' 'Ark'."
It would be fun, I had to admit, and my 'Oppo' had such charm...
I decided to do it. After all, it could do nobody harm.

I knew the 'Reds' had a man in space- and the 'Yanks' were chasing Glory:
What I didn't know was that what I knew was only half the story.
Our 'Top Brass' down in Plymouth, claiming plans were now complete
To combat cramped conditions, for the comfort of the Fleet,
Had asked the 'Yards' to build a ship which had a lot of space;
But what was launched sent blushes round the Plymouth Naval Base.
The need had been misunderstood; the builders made a slip
And now the Navy owned the world's first Very-much-spaceship!

Well, yes, it had to be hushed up: the 'Crabs' would surely crow...
And I was so far down the list - I didn't need to know!

So now I sit in this crater, looking up at the Earth, in the sky,
With this bubble of glass and bottle of air and the hint of a tear in my eye.
I can still just see the receding form of the rocket which brought me here;
Which cast me adrift with a parting gift of a 'Tot' and a crate of beer.

The Drafting Office, bless their hearts, had really called my bluff.
I got no more than I deserved! Old 'Drafty' could be tough.
Still! Better make the most of it! The Yanks'll be here soon...
I wonder if they have an 'Aggie Weston's' on the Moon.

Naturally we sailors learned, quite quickly, how to beat the system. If the last place on Earth you wanted to be at was Lossiemouth, that would be your first choice on the form!

I mentioned Netta Day. What a fascinating lady she is; an absolute bundle of fun. Joan asked her, out of a natural inquisitiveness, "What, exactly, did you do for the sailors?"
Netta grinned, from ear to ear, replying, "Everything!"
Make of that what you will! Having been a sailor, I might have just taken it the wrong way!

Opposite - **Moon**

Living and working, as I do, in a magnificently beautiful part of the World, like so many others, I suppose, I become selfishly inhospitable towards those hoards of holidaymakers who descend upon us throughout the Summer. Twice before I've written somewhat denigratingly about 'Them'.

And I'm not the only one... Come on! There is a hypocrite lurking inside each and every one of us... Yes there is! We all grumble about the 'Touristas' but, if one of them happens to be young, female and 'topless', there wouldn't be a murmur from the males amongst us. So I philosophize...

"The Sun Worshippers"

There are those who go down to the seaside
To build sandcastles, high in the air:
There are those whose sole aim
Is for Guiness Book fame
For the length of a sit in a chair.

There are those who go down to the seaside
For some innocent paddling about:
There are those who go down
To get just forearms brown
And some others who cast ne'er a clout.

But the ones who I find most compelling
Are the ladies who worship the Sun,
Who go out on the sand,
Suntan lotion in hand,
And just roast until everything's done!

My colleagues and I, and our boss, Captain Ted, must ever suffer the frustrations of holiday makers who don't know the rules, boaters who break the rules and a parliament whose members seem to think no rules are necessary.

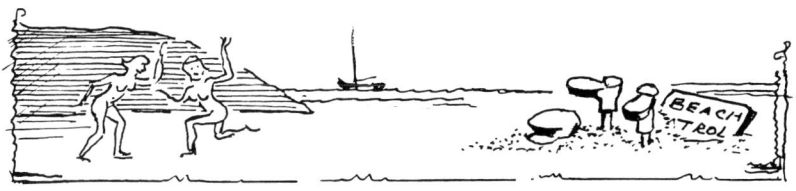

If you don't poke fun at it, from time to time, the situation could become stressful.

"The Black Rock Bad Guys"

"We must take control of these boaters,"
Said my boss, one day, sat at his desk.
"Slap a summons or two on their motors!
Their behaviour is really grotesque!"

He rose and we headed for Black Rock
Where a car was seen breaking the rules
And another was stuck, on the tide-line,
With the occupants waving like fools.

We were walking, now, down to the foreshore.
"Micro-lights are forbidden," he said.
It was then, as I fondly remember,
A seagull did its 'biz' on his head!

"Topless bathing is out of the question;
Not to mention it's extremely rude!"
When we'd entered the beach, at the West end,
I'd seen several young girls in the nude!

Without doubt the frustration was biting:
He referred to 'The Ultimate Sin'.
He threw up his hands in despair,
Saying, "Tell me! Where does one begin?"

Feeling guilty, I offered my service.
"I promise you, I'll do my best!
Let me handle these topless sun-bathers,
Leaving you to look after the rest!"

I could see that he wasn't delighted!
If murder had never been banned
I'd have finished up, later that evening,
Buried several feet deep in the sand.

He's a super fellow really. We all think the world of him!

And, on a more serious note, what about this!

Linos E Leat, a garden gnome with extra special talents, was despatched from Salisbury to Porthmadog with instructions to involve himself in the activities of the local people and to report his progress, by post, back to his mistress.

Heather Leat is a bedridden lady whose lifestyle has been improved, quite dramatically, by her own family and by the Salisbury Lions Club.

Heather loves her garden. Her husband rigged up a series of mirrors, so that she could see her favourite section, the goldfish pond, which is attended by some very loyal and conscientious guards. No stone is left unturned, as they say.

Then, one day, one of the Gnomes, Linos, was absent from place of duty. Heather was very sad. No one seemed to be able to throw light upon his disappearance. Several days went by. The family feared the worst... he had been Gnome-napped.

But no! Linos was on his way around the U.K., and soon the letters and postcards were on their way back to Heather.

By the time he arrived in Porthmadog, Linos had obviously heard about this strange harbourmaster who 'laid' buoys, wrote poetry and couldn't turn down a request! So he asked if he could stay with Joan and me. The Porthmadog Lions, who had sponsored his trip to North Wales, agreed on the understanding that his correspondence with Heather, from here, should rhyme!

Linos came downstream with Dafydd and me to 'lay' No 8 buoy. Subsequently he wrote the following letter which he wouldn't let me see... but which I was able to crib by that age-old method of rubbing a soft pencil over the backing paper he had used in the typewriter.

Aren't I a rotten sneak?

He had said:-

Dear Heather,

You may be quite surprised to see my current turn of phrase.
   They tell me even gnomes are writing poems, these days.
It's all the fault of Michael, the Lion with whom I stay.
   He roused my interest and then said he'd show me the way.

Up from the plains of Salisbury, into the peaks of Wales,
   I came to seek adventure- and found no more than gales.
They told me, at the border, that I wouldn't feel a thing;
   That all a Welshman ever does is play rugby, and sing.
It isn't true, I'll tell you! Just like the Lions back home,
   These Taffs were very eager to impress your wandering gnome.
They'd heard about my expertise with knots and rope and chain
   And asked if I would help them with a job- out on the 'Main'.
Well, Heaven knows I'm seasick if the goldfish splash about-
   The thought of going in a boat left me in lots of doubt!
The Harbourmaster, though, I like. He has a heart of gold.
   When they cast him, I'm bound to say, they surely broke the mould;
And he was so persuasive that I just could not refuse;
   So here I am to tell you all my 'fascinating' news!

We set off early, one March morn', the weather a bit 'iffy'.
  The Skipper said, "Don't worry, Chum, we'll be back in a jiffy!"
I wish I hadn't listened. We sailed around for hours
  In waves that he called 'Little lumps', and I called 'Eiffel Towers'!
And all to place a little buoy... 'he' said, "To mark the channel."
  I don't know what you think, but I say that's a load of flannel...
'Cos when the job was over, and I thought we'd come back in,
  Out came the rods and line and bait! Yuk! Maggots in a tin!

They weren't bad blokes though, really. The Mate was quite a chap!
  I got on very well with him. Twas he who took the 'snap'.
No need for you to worry, now. I'm safely back on shore;
  And, though they did invite me, I will not go any more.
It was a good experience. The scenery was grand...
  But, all the while it lasted, I just longed to be on land!

So, now you know! I'm hopeless as a sailor on the seas!
  I think I'll stick to garden ponds, to flowers, grass and trees.

I promise I'll write a proper letter when Michael isn't around. He gets so 'up-tight' if anyone writes prose! I think he's flipped.

Meanwhile, keep your pecker up and, as usual,

   Much Love,   Linos.

He enclosed the photograph taken by Dafydd, of himself perched on the top of No 8, where we threatened to leave him, stranded, if he didn't stop moaning.

Later, he did write a proper letter... and sent several post cards. I hope it gave Heather some 'Diversion'.

Is it senile dementia, or is it simply that I enjoy a good laugh? One or other of these diagnoses causes me, from time to time, to do stupid things without so much as a passing thought for the consequences.

Like when I saw young Mike Quinnell playing with his model yacht (I don't know that 'playing' is necessarily the right word... He was deadly serious!), I couldn't resist sending him a bill for Harbour Dues.

Poor Mike! He claimed in his response, that it had taken him considerable thought to determine whether or not this was a joke. At the 'going rate', his three feet long yacht 'Spondicious', would have cost him £15.54, plus mooring rental and 'Launch fee'.

"Will I have to negotiate a bank loan?" he asked himself.

Then he had a bright idea. To stab back at the Harbourmaster, send him a poem! And, if you really want to hurt him, to twist the knife, as it were, make a donation to one of his favourite charities.

He wrote:-

"Harbour Dues, Porthmadog- For All"

On this fine morn' of April sixth, I sipped my cup of tea.
   The cheery postman brings the mail. Hurrah! There's one for me!
Porthmadog postmark on the stamp, a hand I seem to know,
   I fumble with the envelope- What's this? A bill? Oh no!

My model yacht 'Spondicious', it's only three feet long;
   Yet I must pay full fifteen pounds to join the boating throng.
There's more- a launching fee. Oh dear! It really can't be true,
   And even mooring fees, as well, to add to harbour dues.

I shuffled through the coloured forms of jargonistic prose,
   Depression on my furrowed brow- but then a thought arose.
From my interpretation, it seems quite plain to me
   That if no mooring is required... then neither is a fee!

But then a pang of conscience comes; I think of the displays
   That line the walls of the Museum, to tell of bygone days.
So, Harbourmaster, please accept a little gift to go
   Towards the harbour history... to help the ebb and flow!

No way was I going to let him get away with that! Diabolical sauce, I called it!

I replied:-

Harbour Dues- My Reply

Mr M. R. Quinnel- 'Spondicious'

Dear Sir,

   I thank you for your note- and rhyme.
   It seems I've committed a crime!

Because I'm such a pleasant bloke
I seldom ever need to joke,
So when I sent your Harbour Bill
  (Which, seemingly, made you quite ill)
There was no motive other than
  To prove you are an honest man;
If proof were needed, which I doubt!
  The Quinnell kindness just floods out!

Your explanation I admire,
Expressed with verve and flair and fire.

My boss said, "OK. 'Stem' your greed!
  But keep a close eye on his speed.
Proportionately it should be
  No more than half a knot, you see!"

Well, there you go, my fine young friend:
  You know, now, we're all round the bend.

Your 'fiver', though, is safe and sound.
  We thank you, muchly, pound by pound
And hope your season's full of fun!

It's only the first round you've won!!!

       Yours sincerely,   ... And I signed it, of course.

    That lovely lady who used to produce the Madoc News, very kindly included both of these letters in the May 1990 issue: so, if you have read them, already, I do apologise. The fact is that I hope there are thousands of you, out there, reading this book, who have absolutely no idea what Madoc News is...   No offence intended, Penny! or Glen!

I listened, the other day, to an interview on radio, of a man, whose name I refuse to remember, who claimed to be a scientist and yet was inflexible, to the point of rigidity, in his denial of even the slightest possibility of the existence of 'extra-terrestrial' life.

How anyone can be so pedantic in the face of such overwhelming probability, I cannot imagine. Does any Earthling have the right to believe that his planet, representing only one electron of one atomic fragment of the Universe, carries the only collection of chemicals capable of supporting life?

This precept is utter nonsense!

As I've said before, I receive a lot of poetry, through the post, from people who wish to help me with the compilation of these books. I am very grateful to them.

As if to support my belief in 'Extra Terrestrials', the following piece arrived in the Interplanetary mail, Star-dated and postmarked 'Sevenda Trid'. It's a good job I don't understand their monetary system. Ten Credits may not sound a lot, but I bet it cost a fortune in postage!

The accompanying letter was in Sevendian. (I am so glad I paid attention in Star School.) It said, "You are welcome to use this in your next book of poems, if you think it is up to your high standard." I tell you! Flattery will get you everywhere!

"Extra Terrestrials"

"On a far off planet, not dissimilar to Earth,
A female of their species was preparing to give birth.
She wasn't breathing 'gas-and-air', as earthly women might,
But having had six kids before, she wasn't paled with fright.

She opened up the vital place at her God-given time
And out popped a bambino in a 'new born' coat of slime.
She checked to see if all was well, and everything was there -
Two heads, four arms, six legs and not a blemish anywhere.

Then, turning to her husband who, as master of the house,
Had made his mind up that the boy should be called Micky Mouse,
She said, "Hey, Man! I'm curious to know, for what it's worth,
I wonder if they go through all this business down on Earth!"

Sorry! All you ladies! Just a bit of fun!

One chap I know who would never be pedantic or, in any way opinionated. I bet Don Winterman believes in Life beyond the Solar System.

The only thing I have against him is that he writes better poetry than I.... but then, he it is who lives on Shakespeare Drive!

When Joan and I were married, one of our congratulatory cards was from Don and his wife, Judy. Wouldn't you know it, it included the following rhyme:-

"A Wedding Congratulation"

If you've read "P.G.Woodhouse" as I'm sure you must have done,
Of the sayings at the Drone's Club, you will recall this one -
That when a chap gets married, and they recover from the shock,
The other fellows liken it to "Jumping off the Dock"
Now I know that, two short years ago, you didn't jump, you fell,
And you know that we're delighted that, once more, you're fit and well.
So, when I heard that you were jumping off the dock again,
I thought, at first, "This fellow really must enjoy the pain!"
But putting all this merry sport and frolicking aside
(As you must if you're determined to take yourself a bride!)
I need to strike a wiser note and truly I do pray
You'll recognise the sincerity in what I'm about to say.

Unlike boats, all restless men, throughout this restless realm,
Are better steered through life's rough seas with a woman at the helm.
And you may ask me, Mike, my friend, how I know this to be true:
What answer can I give you?? since Judy will read this, too!!

So, as you sail through the sea of life, through storm and tempest too,
There'll be many times when you thank God for your wise choice of crew.
With all sincerity I wish, as you dodge those oil slicks,
For calmest seas and fairest winds - for you and Mrs. Bicks.

Wasn't that lovely of him?

Those of you lucky enough to have read Volume Two may recall how Don wheedled his way into Porthmadog harbour by the deft use of rhyming words. Now, of course, he is an established and well loved member of the P.T.S.C. who makes a valuable contribution to the harbour and, it seems, to the Sailing fraternity as a whole.

Having started my friendship with Don through his request for a mooring, I am now receiving requests from fellows who he is teaching... teaching what? To sail, to navigate... or to wheedle their way on to my moorings?

Perhaps he is teaching them to write poetry!

Don failed to return his 'Yellow' Mooring Confirmation Form, this Winter. Naturally I had to reprimand him... along with several hundred others!

And this was his reply:-

"The Yellow Form"

It serves me right! I am so contrite.
I should have contacted you sooner.
I could blame you not if you'd given my 'trot'
To a Serbo Croatian schooner!

I am in disgrace 'cos I need my place
And should, clearly, have filled in my form
And, if that's not enough, your sharp rebuff
Has made me feel quite forlorn.

I said to myself, "Can I bribe him with wealth?
No! He's too honest for that, if you know him.
So- How can I win? Change his grimace to grin?
He's a sucker, of course, for a poem!"

I'm so sorry, Mike, and I really dislike
The thought that I should offend you.
I've filled in my form, for fear of your scorn,
And this, with apologies, send you.

                                        Cheers, Don.

All over the page were little blots of a pinkish brown hue. The postscript explained:-

P.S.

It should be understood that those spots are not blood
Caused by my pain and disgrace.
I'm attending my mail with some good Ruddles ale
And I've spilled it all over the place!

I must confess I didn't know he was a drinking man. It could explain a lot! See what you think of his following epic. It was 'commissioned', I should explain!

"Frank Shala- And the Powerboat Men"

Recall the Ancient Mariner:
He had a tale to tell.
Well, I'll relate another
That will stir you just as well.

    Frank Clark he was a sailing man,
    A sailing man was he!
    His second love was the salt sea spray...
    His first was a 'cuppa tea'.

Young Jackie was his daughter,
The star of his family crew.
He taught her the art of seamanship-
And he taught her how to brew!

One day he was a working hard
On the engine of his boat
And Jackie was brewing a 'cuppa'
To soothe his parching throat.

Then, just as Jackie was pouring
Hot water into the pot,
A speedboat roared by Shala
And spilled the bloody lot.

Young Jackie she was scalded.
Frank's rage was plain to see;
For cruel fate had unfolded
A blow to his crew- and his tea!

Many years have passed since then,
But our hero never forgot
To be wary of fast motor boats
As you steep the P.G. in your pot.

And so it was, one day, there came
An official looking craft
With sinister men, identically clad
In wet-suits, from fore to aft.

They raced right close by Shala.
At first Frank held his tongue.
He thought they were checking radios
And licence he had none!

But, when they surged right back again
It was more than he could take.
"There's a speed limit in this harbour," he said,
"That you really mustn't break!"

"We are the brave Coastguard," they said.
"We've come to allay your fear."
"Then go and guard some other coast!
We don't want you buggers here!"

Thus it was that Frank became
The guardian of the trots
Against those vulgar power boats
That threaten our tea pots.

And all was calm and peaceful,
As <u>most</u> obeyed the rules,
For them that erred knew Fearless Frank
Would expose them all as fools.

But, latterly, there chanced to come,
Into our spot serene,
The biggest bloody power boat
That you have ever seen!

The boat was full of yuppies
And dolly-birds galore,
Sucking back the G and T's
And calling out for more.

With her Volvo Pentas roaring
And her merry-making crew,
She planed past Frank, on Shala,
As he poised with his Typhoo.

The rage with which he shouted
His command that she should stop
Had skippers throttling back their boats
from Dale to Abersoch!

In truth, our poor offender
Was a lubber of the land.
He did not know what he had done;
He did not understand.

"I am a film director,"
Said this affable young chap.
"You buggers are all the same," said Frank,
"So don't give me that crap!"

The poor young fellow tried again.
With remorse he was beset:
But Frank had lost his 'cuppa'!
He wasn't finished yet!

But when, at last, he paused for breath
From hurling his derision,
It slowly dawned on him... the chap
Really was from television.

"What is the nature of your task?"
Asked Frank, with cynical note.
"A film for Welsh TV," he replied,
"On Safety for Children Afloat." ! !

Don (Bless him!) apologises for the use of some 'naughty' words. He did suggest some alternatives but felt that the poem would have 'lost' something if diluted. I have to agree with his sentiment, but would add... There is so much there, Don, old chap, that it could afford to lose 'something' and would still be great.

Opposite - **Power Boats**

Early in this book I mentioned Stephen Townsend and the discussions he and I have had on Modern versus Traditional art forms.

Stephen once said, "I just can't see, no matter how many 'O' or 'A' levels a person may have or how intellectual they may be; whether they come from Eton or East Ham, how the Hell can anybody make any sense out of a piece of metal or a painting which bears no resemblance to anything on Earth- or in space come to that!

I reckon these so-called Modern Artists have carved themselves out their own little 'niche' in the market in an attempt to bewilder us with a load of old garbage, so as to earn themselves a few 'bob'.

Some people will pretend their intelligence to be on a higher plane than that of us ordinary folk. If they make some daft explanation about a totally unexplainable object, who am I to try to stop them? I just wonder who's kidding who: is it the artists or their admirers?".

I am reminded of that old story about the lady who arrested her husband's somewhat inelegant haste through a gallery, to bid him share with her the beauty of one of the paintings.

The canvas was almost totally black. There was one small, circular, yellow blob in the top, right hand corner. "There!" the lady pointed. "That says it all for me".

The man grunted in resignation.

"Can't you just feel it," the lady went on. "There you have the darkness of total despair; the blackness of evil night, the desolation of loneliness... and yet... the vaguest hint of salvation... a promise that somewhere, up there... look! See! A sun is trying to break through. Even in the depths of misery there is Hope... I've got to have it!".

"Alright," said the husband, grabbing a passing attendant. "How much is that one?"

The attendant walked over to the painting, peeled off the yellow blob and looked at it. "Two hundred guineas, Sir," he said.

I think it fair to say that, in the final analysis, Stephen and I agree that beauty is in the eye of the beholder.

I get 'up-tight' when I see a 'poem' such as...

> *All the little children*
> *Run out into the field*
> *To play.*
> *They are smiling.*
> *They are so happy!*

... and an appraisal which purports to be by an expert but which declares... "It is wonderfully evocative!"

It makes me wonder, "Where did I go wrong?"

Stephen, who claims there isn't an ounce of poetry in him, anywhere, has written a couple of short pieces 'to prove it'. The first, I think, shows a high degree of sensitivity and the second only goes to prove that he has not yet made up his mind where religion is concerned.

"My Friend"

*My friend never lets me down
When things are getting rough.
My friend never wears a frown
When things are getting tough.*

*My friend never asks me "Why?"
When I do a silly deed...
My friend never tells a lie
When it's the truth I really need!*

and...

"After"

*What's this thing we call Death?
 Surely we don't just run out of breath!
Whatever it is I think I'll pass.
 I don't really fancy being one of God's Class.*

*Being of Earth suits me swell:
 From what I've heard it's better than Hell;
So, to who ever Judges me in my final hour,
 Just leave me in the ground! I'll prop up a flower!*

I reckon the only thing that Stephen has proved is the truth in saying that a Poet lurks inside every one of us!

* * * * * * * * * * *

There is certainly a poet lurking inside G. E. Garley of Frodsham who sent a card to me in October, 1989. On reflection, I don't think he needed, or wanted anything that I could give him; so his flattery is all the more acceptable. He said,

"An Acknowledgement"

*"How pleasant to know Mr Bicks!
His book's a peculiar mix
 Of this and of that
 And of Percy the cat
And Phantasmagorical tricks.*

*Yes, it's pleasant to know Mr Bicks!
He's written two volumes of 'stuff'
 About aunts and their cars
 And randy Jack Tars...
But there! I have said quite enough."*

In Hilary Roberts (Promises are all I get!) the poet is not so much lurking as smiling all over her face. She has a wonderful sense of humour... so I forgive her for 'picking me up', from time to time, when the minutest of errors slips by, un-noticed.

I thought I had her, though, when Penny Butler published "Why is a Boat Called 'She'?" and 'Old Sharp-eyes' pounced.

She wrote, inside my Christmas card, would you believe...

"A Ticking Off"

"I'll tell you Mikee...

Although well written in
Rhythmic rhyme,
I spotted a 'gaff' in your
Verse, this time.

Me thinks perhaps you were
Missing the 'sea'
When scrolling aquire where
Acquire should be!"

Well! I wasn't going to stand for that, was I! I wrote straight back, thanking the Roberts for their card and explaining that this unforgivable spelling mistake was, of course, a 'Printer's error'!

It was just after that exchange and, no doubt, held up by the Christmas rush, that my own copy of Madoc News arrived. I wonder if they planned it, between themselves...

Penny, bless her heart, had 'Desk-top' published the poem in my own handwriting!

And...

"Why is a Boat Called 'She'?"

I learned, while very young, that boats are always known as 'She':
My father, who was 'Nautical', passed that 'gem' on to me:
But there, among the facts of life, however I may pry,
He never quite came round to giving reasons as to why.

Of course, in later years, when cruising in my father's wake,
I noticed things which rendered this tradition less opaque.
A boat can be contrary, never doing what she should,
And yes, it takes a lot of paint to keep her looking good.

A vessel has a waist, and stays, and gangs of men about;
She causes lots of bustle and can be quite well decked out.
To handle her correctly takes a man with nerves of steel
For she is uncontrollable with no-one at the wheel.

> *It may not cost a fortune to <u>acquire</u> a little boat,*
> But just you watch the pennies go in keeping her afloat!
> She often shows her bottom- but with charm and grace and poise
> And, coming into harbour, makes a beeline for the buoys!
>
> So, now I think I know the facts, my mind may rest at ease;
> I need not feel so chauvinistic charging Harbour Fees.
> It matters not! A boat's a boat... whatever be its sex...
> As years roll by they all become just old, forgotten WRECKS!

Would you have had the courage to read that one to the Abersoch Women's Institute? Having agonized, all over the Christmas holidays, I finally did so on the 20th. of February, 1990... and I am still alive!

* * * * * * * * * * *

The 'meat' of this poem was supplied by Keith S. Jones of Porthmadog, boatman and writer of children's stories... (I do hope that Sandy Mann and Jetsam get into orbit), who invited me to put it into rhyme. I say 'invited' to be kind... 'Challenged' would probably be nearer the mark.

There is only a narrow margin, in my 'Onboard' dictionary, between 'Commission' and 'Challenge', when it comes to writing poetry.

We have, in this parish, some colourful characters, and I wish I had the expertise necessary to bring them to the attention of the outside world. The more famous, the Sea Captains and Industrialists, for instance, are handled by the experts, Aled Eames, Dr. Lewis Lloyd, and so on. The less famous but, nevertheless equally interesting, unfortunately may remain obscured.

One such person was Willie Paul, The Swan Man. Some of you may remember Willie who died, sadly, a few years ago. I owe him for his most expert and unselfish caring of the swans, and other sea birds, while he was alive and capable. Anything I write about him seems inadequate to express my admiration... but I shall keep on trying!

Another 'character' is Bondo. I don't know his real name, (he lied, glibly!) nor the origins of the nickname, but I can tell you he is one of those men one meets, from time to time, who registers, instantly, something about his personality, character, charisma, call it what you will, strikes home.

Bondo has had the odd fishing boat or two but is known to me best as The Drayman, the driver of the Bass Charrington lorry around these parts.

One lunch time, at the Madoc Yacht Club bar (I had gone in on official business, you understand!), Bondo said to me, "You've written poetry about everyone else in the whole world, except me... What have I done to upset you? I know! I'm not important enough...!"

He went on and on. I accepted it as a challenge and wrote the following little 'skit'. I haven't seen him since, so I don't know whether or not he was amused. Again, the fact that I am still alive means either that he didn't bother to read it or that he took it as the joke it was meant to be.

For those who do not have the benefit of the Welsh, I should explain that 'Chwarae teg' means 'Fair play'!

"Bondo"

So this 'bird' sidled up to this fellow,
  Quite the machoest man you'll have seen,
Saying, "How about you being skipper... and crew
  On my yacht, 'M.V. Lovelong Serene'?"

Although taken aback, he responded
  With a nonchalant nod and a preen:
Then he lowered his head and, with dignity, said,
  "My name's Bond... Oh, you must be the Queen!"

"It won't cost you much," she asserted;
  "The one thing I am not is mean.
Just a bit, chwarae teg - well, an arm and a leg
  But I'll leave you your liver and spleen!"

Bondo thought of these harsh implications,
  Realising he wasn't that keen:
So he made up his mind that the courage he'd find
  To admit that he hadn't a bean.

He said, "Madam, you'd better forget it!
  All that eros just isn't my scene.
You may well be a 'dish'... but I'd much rather fish.
  I'm a soup-plate! I'm not a tureen!"

Where would we be without the Bondos and the Willie Pauls of this world... or, indeed, the Keith Scott Joneses?

* * * * * * * * * *

Keith's daughter, Ilona Sarita Jones- What a lovely name- has written what I recognise as a plea from the heart. I don't suppose, for one moment, that 'Daddy' will recognise it as such. Well, he's a hard man!

At age thirteen, Ilona has penned:-

"A Boat Would be Good"

My Daddy is a 'nutter';
  (I won't reveal his name).
He's not rich and has no boat,
  But I love him, just the same.

The very crucial factor
  That he doesn't own a yacht
Doesn't change my mind
  And I still love him a lot.

But, as I think again,
  A boat could be so good.
Do I still love him?
  Well, I SUPPOSE I should!

Maybe I will ask him
  If we can have a yacht.
Then I think I'll love him
  Not a bit- but quite a lot!

It does and old codger like me a power of good to see such efforts coming from a young teenager.

Yes! Old codger... That's me! And my degenerating memory is here to prove it. Do you know, for Christmas, 1989, Joan bought me a book called "Total Recall". The purpose was to help me to regain those lost moments... and I can't, for the life of me, remember where I put it!

I sometimes don't do things for the oddest of memorial reasons. I remember that something has to be done, but for geographical or practical reasons it is, instantly, undo-able: so I forget it again. Then it never gets done because I remember remembering that it had to be done but forget forgetting to do it... and so I think that it has been done!

* * * * * * * * * * *

One such oddity is this next poem. I remember writing it down somewhere other than on a scrap of paper. It isn't, so far, in this book. It isn't in Diversion 1 or 2, so where is it? How frustrating! How, often, embarrassing.

I do remember explaining that the blank space is to be filled by the reader with any name which seems appropriate... and has only one syllable.

We start with an old proverb...

"Patience"

Patience is a virtue- possess it if you can.
It's often found in women but seldom in a man.

Patience is a virtue whose rewards are there to reap;
But when you have a ...... around, its difficult to keep.

Patience is a luxury enjoyed by those with time!
For youngsters, then, to lose it must surely be a crime!

But when you get to my age; when time is running out,
The whole concept of patience must be held in deepest doubt.

So when I ask a favour or demand a job be done,
Get to it... if you have a mind to see tomorrow's Sun!

Who said I'm a bad-tempered old rascal? Well, you're probably right! And I have been called worse things!

* * * * * * * * * * *

I wonder what my grandson muttered, under his breath, when his birthday came, and went, without so much as a card from 'Taid'.

It was during the Postal Dispute, I hasten to explain. I had sent a card, with cheque inside, but it was clearly held up by Industrial Action.

You know how it is... I was waiting for a 'Thank-you' letter, muttering things like... "I don't know! Kids... these days...!" when I received a note from his Mum saying that David would 'Let me off' if I sent him a poem, instead of a card. Oh God! Another commission!

I wrote...

"David's Birthday Card"

So David wants a little rhyme, does he?
Well, if we can we'll make the time, won't we!

I'd like to know the dreadful fate
Of the card I sent, which is very late,
And which, caught up in the Postman's brawl,
May never arrive at 'yours' at all.

It's easy to blame poor Postman Pat
But I know I sent it! I'm sure of that
And further, I'd publicly announce
That if he dropped it- the cheque would bounce!

No! I jest and I hope and pray, my lad
That your birthday was one of the best you've had.
Now, when it arrives, give this cheque to your Mum
And tell her, if she doesn't come up with the cash,
toute de suite,
I'll smack her... bottom

We still don't know what happened to the original.
                        The cheque was never cashed!

* * * * * * * * * * *

Kids! Have you noticed? They're either little horrors... or little angels. There seems to be a vast chasm of emptiness between these extremes: or is it just me!?

One of the angels, I suspect, is Emma Grayson. Now I have not had the pleasure of meeting Emma but her grandfather has been to see me, a couple of times, to talk about poetry and to mention that "Emma has written a few lines".

You know me! The original sceptic! Oh God! Another doting grandparent!

Also the original hypocrite! I have said some awful things about the 'Modern' style of non-rhyming poetry; blank verse, or whatever they call it.

I have 'knocked' it- and I have written it... and now I am going to ask your indulgence, indeed beg your criticism of some of Emma's work. Perhaps I should tell you, before you read on, that Emma Grayson was only eight years old when she wrote:-

"Christmas Gifts"

The Bulgy, strong, brilliant tree
Waits with patience
Till Christmas day
With burdens on its branches.
Gifts.
Gifts which we need,
Gifts loved all over the world,
Invisible gifts
Like strength, health and courage
And visible gifts
When Jesus was alive.
Gold, frankincense and myrrh
Were given by the rich.
Sheepskins, crooks and wool
Were given by the shepherds and poor.
But we must not forget
The disabled, homeless, starving and poor.
They, too, need a Happy Christmas like me;
So do the soldiers in Saudi Arabia.
But the bulging, strong, brilliant tree
Can provide confidence, courage and
Strength to the world.
It can bring a present to everyone.

The period during which that deep, philosophical appreciation of the Christmas spirit was composed is indicated by the mention of the soldiers in Saudi.

I am truly impressed. That a girl of her age should be aware of the events unfolding in the Middle East is notable: to have an empathetic recognition of the participants' need for a Happy Christmas shows a maturity beyond her years. Let's face it- I was only a year younger when, in 1940, I thought the Far East to be "The other side of 'Dagenham'".

I have some more of Miss Grayson's work with which I shall startle you later on.

Meanwhile more confessions...

I was talking to one of my cats, this morning. He had just 'limped' into the bedroom and clawed his way on to the bed like a tired old man. I said, "For Christ's sake, Cat! What have you been up to?"

He sort of grunted and licked a paw.

That cat is seven years old. Now I don't know the facts but, looking at it logically, a cat-year seems to me to be about seven human-years... so he is only forty nine.

I said, "You've a while to go yet before... before what? Where do cats go when they 'pop their clogs'?"

I could see he was violently interested in this conversation by the way he curled up and closed his eyes.

"Is it to that Great Cat's Home in the Sky?" I persisted. "It's a long, long way up... but I'm told it's Heaven when you get there."

I am fond of cats, as you may have guessed... anybody's cats... but my own trio, two strays and a 'was going to be put down' are extra special.

"Cats- Taff"

The winner of the Nobel Prize
  For Lassitude, and doleful eyes;
For being such a gentle bloke
  Who tells you when, and where, to stroke;
For humbling the mere riff-raff...
  It has to be the ponderous Taff!

Plain cat-food is no good for him.
  He must think humans pretty dim
For all he needs to do is point...
  He knows the 'fridge' contains the 'joint'.
A churlish, but demanding pout
  Brings yesterday's left-overs out.

He's dull, predictive, serious;
  No sense of humour- makes no fuss.
In fact he's sometimes good as gold
  So long as we do as we're told!
But, should we run right out of liver,
  He'll give a remonstrative quiver
Then... through the gap- the slimy toad-
  To his other home... just down the road.

"Cats- Cunningham"

Now Cunningham is quite a cat!
  His Mum and Dad made sure of that...
Of all the local Toms and Queens
  They had those very special genes
Which, when combined in kittenhood,
  Had several facets which were good
But, equally, it seems they had
  Some traits which proved to be quite bad.

Though Cunningham may be uncouth
  He says no more than tells the truth.
His honesty, while misconstrued
  By critics who have harshly viewed
His flicky tail, his head-up stance,
  The stretched out paw, the furtive glance,
Is obvious to those who know
  The sting which follows every blow;
The blood which trickles from his claws,
  The permanently grinning jaws...
The poor mouse, laying on the mat!
  He's honestly... a wicked cat!!

"Cats- Daisy"

*Young Daisy may yet come up 'trumps'.
She is the one who hops and jumps.
She joined us as a little waif
And now no hiding place is safe:
The wardobe top, the kitchen sink-
You'll lose your breakfast, if you blink,
For she is hungry, night and day.
When other cats just want to play.
Or settle, purring, on your lap
To watch 'the box' or have a nap,
You'll hear her meow, but pay no heed;
She only wants another feed!*

*If you ignore her plaintive cry
She'll catch, and scoff, a butterfly.
Then, if you still don't meet her terms,
She'll even dig up garden worms.
Yet she is glossy, slender, sleek
And full of almost-human cheek.
It's no use feeding verbal flak
To Daisy! She just answers back!*

*She's young. She has a lot to learn
And lots of midnight oil to burn.
Though outwardly she plays 'The Brute'...
We think she's really rather cute!*

* * * * * * * * * *

I've always been a believer in 'Fair play', particularly within the family unit. You know... Like when Dad treats himself to a new PWP, or Personal Word Processor, the very least Mum should expect is the right to a new PRP or Pastry Rolling Pin.

So, in keeping with this principal, I have tried to be fair in that I have attempted to write appraisals of the other members of the family - in a similar idiom:-

"Cats- Lyn and Joan"

You've heard of 'Alternative' this
And you've heard of 'Alternative' that!
Well, we have a creature called Lyn
Who is an 'Alternative' cat!

But

Of all the feline creatures which scat around this house,
The one I love the most is really just a little mouse.
She prances on her hind legs, to dust the mantlepiece,
And drives the vacuum cleaner like a flock of hissing geese.

In spite of what her husband says, she's not a 'silly moo';
In fact her grammar is as good as that of 'me and you'.
Were I a lion tamer I would tame this lioness...
But no! I play the Jester to her Regal Good Queen Bess!

... And, talking of lions... well, they are cats, aren't they...! And, dare I mention the occasional tin-shaking I do, on behalf of the RNLI, the Girl Guides and countless other worthy causes...

"Mrs Bouquet"

I met Mrs. Bucket, the other day,
Who said, with impatience, "No! It's Bouquet!
Now I'm very busy, so state your intent!
If it's Oxfam my gift has already been sent."

Then she saw my badge. "Oh, you're one of those!
Well, I may spare a couple of pence, I suppose."
I thought she was going to ask me in.
Instead she just dusted the top of my tin.

"My husband's a Ma... " she started to brag.
I thought, yeah! I bet! You silly old ha...
Ha... half a crown will do nicely... Thank you very much!

* * * * * * * * * *

It is not until one declares an intention, to oneself, to become a successful poet, that one discovers how many countless thousands of other people nurture the same ambition.

Wouldn't you think, especially after the ridicule attached by a certain, doughy T.V. series, that most 'normal' people would keep their poetic tendencies under wraps. Not a bit of it! I heard that a recent poetry competition which required an entry fee of £15, per poem, had attracted over 4,500 entries. The first prize was £75 and there were several 'runner-up' prizes. Alright! Lets say there were a total of £500 worth of prizes. That still leaves £67,000 to cover costs, etc. I think, perhaps, that I am on the wrong side of the typewriter!

* * * * * * * * * * *

Someone else who is clearly in the wrong business is Alan Windsor.

Here is a man of immense talent who combines a near magical insight into nature with an ability to draw compelling word pictures, which I have learned only to envy!

Alan's book "Verse Across the Years" is well worth reading. He has allowed me to 'borrow' from it and has written a couple of pieces for me to 'consider' for this book. My one criticism is, "How the Hell do you do it, Alan?"

"The Weeping Willow"

She is weeping by the banks of flowing rivers,
Born of the loveliness of years;
She is weeping for the precious hopes we cherish
And will wash the barren valley with her tears.

She is weeping in the forests of creation,
Wherein the threads of known Life first began.
The willow weeps in anger and frustration
At the folly and the ignorance of Man.

She is weeping for her many kindred sisters,
Aware of all the dying and the dead.
She is weeping , too, that Man may still awaken,
For Nature's fragile cloak is torn and shred.

She is weeping for the children of the future,
May they yet see the beauty we have known;
Or will she be the symbol of our sorrow
To flower upon the silent Earth alone.

I find myself agreeing with just about everything Alan Windsor says; but if there were no exception, there wouldn't be a rule.

His choice of sex leaves me cold! No, you rude person, not that kind! In his next poem Alan refers to the most majestic piece of flora ever to grace the woodlands of the world, as female. Now I am not a male chauvinist pig... but! There has to be a limit!

"The Oak Tree"

A wind-tossed tiny acorn, it fell, I know not where;
Untroubled by Man's footsteps, 'twas awakened by a prayer.
Ever straight and sturdy, year by year it grew
To flower upon a Springtime that bore all Life anew.

She flourished but in majesty, as gracious as a queen;
While Nature dressed her branches in yellow, gold and green.
Came Knights, adorned in armour, the lonely and the brave,
While vagabonds and pilgrims rested 'neath her shade.

She has seen the weary traveller, the peasant at the plough,
As statesmen, kings and captains have passed 'neath her bough.
She has furnished hearth and homestead, she has weathered every breeze,
And gave her boughs that England might guard the Seven Seas.

She has seen our ancient heritage, how earthly shadows cast
Upon each falling leaf, now but a memory of the past.
So, let us all remember how that tiny acorn grew
To become a mighty Oak Tree, Nature's precious gift to you.

He has that special touch, don't you think! It is a lot easier to just ramble on or to poke fun at some thing.

My final accolade, (to Alan Windsor,) is a sorrowful scan across North America which could easily bring tears to the eyes...

"Red Indian Tragedy"

From the Colorado mountains
 To the windswept Kansas plains
Sounds an ancient war cry of
 A people, still in chains;
Calling back the Blackfeet,
 The Mohawks and the Sioux,
Back to the greatness
 Of a land that they once knew.

Across the wide Missouri
 Where the Cheyenne hunt no more
And the spirits of the Cherokees
 Flow down the Shenandoah,
Wigwams, torn and empty,
 No squaw or little one:
Forlorn still lies the landscape
 For the buffalo have gone.

Through the fading shadows
 The winds of hope still sigh
With the light of ghostly camp fires
 Transfigured in the sky.
Beyond the Little Bighorn,
 His warriers wild and free,
Sitting Bull awaited
 His date with destiny.

Behold the Painted Desert,
 Carved by a mystic hand,
Where the sorrow of a nation
 Lies written in the sand.
Man's crime against his Brother
 Still lingers in the gloom
To leave a thousand heartbreaks
 Beneath the prairie moon.

Opposite - ***Red Indian Tragedy***

Well, I did warn you! That is emotional thinking. It may take a bit of frivolity to ease your anguish; though I would not wish to detract from Alan's deep insight into the vast damage caused to a culture by the arrival of a so-called 'civilization'

The mention of Red Indians, and brothers, reminds me of the tale my brother told of how his teacher, at school, persuaded the class to remember a certain essential, mathematical fact.

It seems a Red Indian Chief lived in a wigwam with a cow-hide laid on the ground as a bed. He took himself a squaw and she gave him a handsome son.
The squaw was not happy with the cowhide bed. Her pleading went unrewarded so she took to threats- "No more 'hanky' 'till the bed is changed!"
The Chief accepted defeat. He went hunting, came back with a buffalo hide... and his squaw gave him another son.
Unfortunately the seeds of doubt had been sown. The relationship was never the same. They agreed on a trial separation... and the Chief fell irretrievably in love with a beautiful young maiden. He ditched the buffalo hide, went hunting and came back with a hippopotamus hide.
Almost instantly, his new squaw bore him twin boys- which only goes to prove that 'The squaw on the hippopotamus is equal to the sons of the squaw on the other two hides!'

Sorry! Perhaps I should not be frivolous!

It is not easy to do justice to aspects of Nature or to describe 'Life' in the raw, as it were.
I tried, once, many years ago. Some of you may recall a poem I wrote about Hong Kong. It was in two parts. I was quite pleased with Part 1 but, though it had to be written, Part 2 was not so satisfying.

What is not generally known, I think, is that 'Hong Kong' was published in a newspaper, in the colony, while I was safely out at sea, and apparently caused a near riot.

Part 1 was published, separately, in a Naval 'Commission' book... and what I am really boasting about is that it enjoyed a fairly wide distribution around the Far East.

Eventually, someone in Singapore, an ex-patriot Brit, took umbrage and insisted that I should write something about that place.

The same horror overtook me as has done all through when commissioned to do some work. Well, you know my feelings on that score! I worried about it, a lot, making notes and even writing a preliminary poem.

Singapore was on the verge of independance. I actually flew out of Singapore on the day that Independence was declared.

"The Requirement"

So much already written, so many words of rhyme,
By oh so many people, who seemed to have the time;
That who am I to question, to praise or to deplore
The many, varied histories of this island, Singapore!

I'm asked to give opinions and to give them all in verse;
A sombre sonnet on Singapore? I can think of nothing worse.
This land deserves the talent of a better man than I,
A writer born but yesterday, tomorrow doomed to die!

However, since but cowardice would keep me from this task
I'll do it, but, of readers, I would this favour ask:
If you find my laboured style is strident to the ear
Then tear this up and burn it! Promise, Reader Dear?

Not many people will have seen Singapore as I did, but then, not many people see anything the way I do so it doesn't bother me a great deal.

This island was an old woman carrying the ageless burden of time. In independence she gave birth to a healthy babe whose future depended on heredity and up-bringing, as in any human child.

Here was the immense love of a man (Lee Kwan Yoo) for a Nation and his drive to spur, into the masses, the same pride in Nationalism, the multi-racial selfness, the coagulation of colours and creeds, living together in semi-harmony, needing but a spark to kindle the flame of intolerance, hatred and violence.

What would be the future of Singapore?

In June, 1967, I wrote...

"Singapore- On Independence"

Breast withered, toothless shell of fragile bones,
Seeking to retain your lost hormones;
To recapture youth, perhaps virginity,
In independent gullibility;
Put not your faith in international power,
Island so small, in this most tender hour;
Race not for arms, in military might,
But show determined, economic fight.

Woman of tired limbs and hideous hide,
Age delitescent in nationalistic pride;
What kind of love has Man for such as thee
That spurs not hatred, multi-racially?
One spark of failure on this troubled road
Of birth, one stumbling 'neath this awesome load
And you will lose your erstwhile passive name
In disillusioned, kampong kindled flame.

To cultivate this 'embryonic' land,
Old woman in confinement, clench your hand
Around the hilt of Life's genetic sword
To cut your Causeway'd umbilical cord.
Alone lies strength, in youthful industry;
Maintaining faith in self identity.
Island of palms and progress, Heaven knows
The World is watching how your Garden grows!

In hindsight, nearly a quarter of a century on, I seem to have been not so far out. Singapore is one of the Financial centres of the world and still has, I believe, the same man at the top.

* * * * * * * * * * *

I bet Singapore is also, still, an idyllic place to be. I had some very memorable moments there... but enough said. I'm not making any more confessions! Well... except I happen to like Slim.
    Here is a lady whose husband, Andrew, obviously adores her and who asked if I would write a few lines in her praise, on his behalf.
    He would only tell me that he calls her Slim. The rest he left to me... another commission! Where will it all end?
    Slim, to me, presents a totally unselfish attitude and has the most warming, winning smile. Oh God! I thought. How may I do her justice? If only I were a real poet! Again I did my best, feeling... knowing that my best is simply not good enough.

"Sunlight in Madog-A Sonnet to Slim"

A miracle, to scare away the night,
Sends rays of Hope to reach across the sky,
To flood the mountains, at the speed of light,
With brightness which would sting the naked eye.

An instant when the depths of dark despair
Are pierced; the bolts of misery are drawn;
The dungeons door, guarding against the glare,
Flies open, and the doubt becomes the dawn.

And that is how I see this lady's smile;
A new awakening to start each day
With warm and kind sincerity, her style
Of friendship on Life's vacillating way.

The boat she rides? A Princess! I declare
The Princess is the lady riding there!

* * * * * * * * * * *

And another confession...

"Sailing for Pleasure"

The sea is flat- we cruise along;
My heart is joyful as a song.
A puff of wind- the sails fill;
I think I'm going to be ill.

In full gale- the poles are bare
And I just died from Mal de Mer!

That is a very personal appraisal of 'Sailing for Pleasure?' I think everyone knows my limitations. Like Linos E Leat Gnome, I get seasick if the goldfish splash about.

Another person whose sailing qualities I have criticised in the past (Volume 1, page 21) is Our Harry. He's a nice enough bloke not to mind... and so I have done it again. The name of his boat is the name of the lyric which is meant to be sung to... well it will become obvious...

"*Immortal Sails*"

The other night he had a dream, the funniest dream of all;
He dreamt he took a little boat out from the harbour wall.
He headed down to Borth y Gest; the sails were pulling taut;
But then he couldn't find his way from there back into Port.

Chorus:

Oh Harry Boy we love you- Harry Boy we love you,
We love you in the Summer, Spring and Fall;
Harry Boy, we love you- Harry Boy, we love you,
The Winter's when we love you most of all!

He sent his wife to evening classes. Gladys did her best;
And now she navigates the trip from Port to Borth y Gest.
Poor girl, she had to learn the lot- the knots, the whips, the splices,
So's Harry could indulge himself in all his little vices.

Chorus:

When Harry plots a course it's like a mess of hairy spiders
So Gladys handles all the charts and fiddles with dividers:
Not only that! She has to have, to satisfy his mewling,
And keep his temper-ature down... a constant teapot brewing!

Chorus:

* Why not have a look at the picture on page 62.

Gladys, bless her heart, has an RYA Coastal Skipper Certificate. Really!
We did another 'fun' thing about Harry, one Christmastime, in the pattern of a popular carol, and as if sung by a 'regal' Customs and Excise Officer.

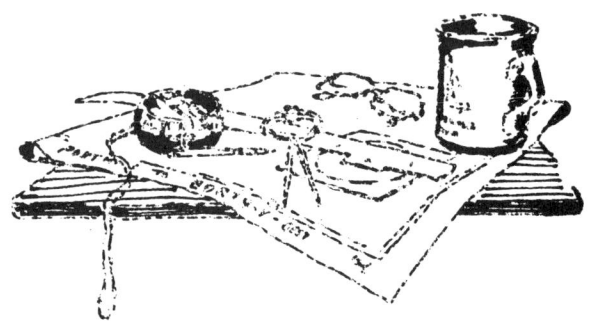

It went...

"A Christmas Carol"

I saw three ships come sailing in,
    On Christmas day, on Christmas day.
I asked them where the Hell they'd been
    On Christmas day, in the morning.

The first one said he'd come from Spain
    On Christmas day, on Christmas day,
And sailed all day in pouring rain
    On Christmas day in the morning.

The second, with a great big smile,
    On Christmas day, on Christmas day,
Said he'd come o'er from Erin's Isle
    On Christmas day in the morning.

The third bloke was a 'canny skip',
    On Christmas day, on Christmas day.
I knew he'd give me lots of 'lip'
    On Christmas day in the morning.

His story, though, I liked the best,
    On Christmas day, on Christmas day,
He said he'd been to "Bord y Gest"
    On Christmas day in the morning.

I can't repeat what Harry said when it was sung at his Christmas dinner: but I'm sure he would not have meant it, anyway!

Harry is somewhere in the middle of life... well... second half, probably. The following few pages are going to be bouncing between the extremes.

I have three very witty appreciations of 'old age' which I shall intersperse with some impressive observations from the younger generation.

I promised more of Emma Grayson. Haven't I raved off about that girl already? I may not be up to some people's standards as a critic, but I know what I like and what I think is good. As I keep on saying, at the risk of being a bore, it is not only the words which are important. The environment in which they were written and, in Emma's case, the age of the writer must be taken into account.

I've tried Miss Grayson's work out on others who, like me, at first were thinking, "Hmm! Not bad for a first year University Student."

"Sounds in the Garden"   by Emma Grayson, Aged Eight.

The wind whistles through my mind
 While the birds are cheeping merrily
In the distance.
 Cars whiz along the road.
Softly I hear the wasp buzzing,
 Quietly.
The trees rumbling and rattling.
 Suddenly, the noise of the grass,
Crackling, popping.

The sound of Kevin's page struck my Ear-
 "Bbbleek", it went.
Meanwhile, I hear
 The soft sound of a dog barking
And the birds singing;
 It made me shake.
The rumbling of the big, huge bus,
 The sudden, gentle sound of lavender
Touching.
 Oh, what's that?
It's the train going along.
 Then the soft, gentle noise of the
Rose petal
 Falling on my toe.
The whole earth shook-
 It's the drill buried in the road.

Then I hear a tap on the ground.
 What is it?
It's a pencil which falls
 On concrete!

I would not have thought of Rosemary as 'old'! She is the lovely, cuddly, engulfing lady who keeps changing cars and gives each new one a name (Volume 2), which then challenges me into writing yet another poem about her latest acquisition.

This time, bless her, Rosemary has done the writing. She has sent the following to me; the first of my geriatric trio.

"Join the Club"

Just a line to say I'm living, that I'm not amongst the dead,
Though I'm getting more forgetful and mixed up in the head.
I've got used to my arthritis, to my dentures I'm resigned;
I can cope with my bifocals, but- Ye gods! I miss my mind!

Sometimes I can't remember, when I'm standing on the stair,
Am I going up for something or have just come down from there?
Before the fridge, so often, my mind is filled with doubt,
Did I come to put food in there, or should I take some out?

If it's not my turn to write, dear, then I hope you won't get sore;
I may think that I have written and don't want to seem a bore.
So remember, I do love you and I wish you lived more near;
Now it's off to mail this letter and say goodbye, my Dear.

As I stand beside the letterbox my face is turning red.
I should have posted this to you... but I've opened it instead!

Ah, yes! I know the feeling. It's like when I call someone on the telephone and, during the conversation, I say something stupid like "Give us your number and I'll call you back" and, while I'm saying it, I'm thinking, "You stupid burke..."

* * * * * * * * *

Now I have no idea, whatsoever, about whom was this next piece written. By whom, yes. It was Gareth, my grandson.

"Three Bad Sailors"

There were three men from Porthmadog
Who decided to sail afar.
When they arrived on dry land,
(Supposedly Ireland),
They found they were at Stranraer!

I'm glad I didn't write it. Any one of those three could turn out to be vicious, unforgiving revengers. But don't worry, Old Son. I won't divulge your address... unless they torture me! No! I would rather you had the opportunity to travel through life, experience its ups and downs and reach the stage currently being enjoyed by Kath Mackenzie...who wrote:-

"My Get-Up-And-Go Has Gone And Went"

How do I know my youth is all spent?
Well, my get-up-and- go has gone and went!
But, in spite of it all, I am able to grin
When I think of where all my 'Get-up' has 'bin'.

"Old age is golden", so I've heard it said,
But, sometimes I doubt as I get into bed;
My ears in a drawer, my teeth in a cup,
My eyes on a table, until I wake up!
Ere sleep dims the rest, I say to myself,
"Is there anything else that should go on the shelf?"

Now don't get me wrong! I'm not jealous or sore.
My friends are the same... and perhaps even more!

When I was young, my slippers were red;
I could kick my heels jauntily over my head.
When I grew older, my slippers were blue;
But still I could dance the whole night through.
Now I am ancient, my slippers are black;
I walk to the stores... and puff my way back.

The reason I know that my youth is all spent...
My get-up-and-go has got-up-and-went:
But I really don't mind, when I think, with a grin
Of all the grand places my 'Get-up' has 'bin'.
Since I have retired from Life's competition
I busy myself with complete repetition.
I get up each morning and dust off my wits,
Then pick up the papers and read the 'Obits'.
If my name is not mentioned, I know I'm not dead,
So I eat a good breakfast... and go back to bed!

How often have I thought, "I wish I'd written that!" All to often, I'm afraid. The more poetry I receive from other writers the more I have to accept that, for any one of us to become 'famous' we are going to have to compete not only with the legacies of Wordsworth, Shelley and so on, but with eachother. It is a sad fact. I think we should go back to the old days when only a privileged few received an education. The competition would be far less... but, knowing my luck, I would be one of the underprivileged masses.

One contender for literary fame has to be Gareth Hickman... If he ever survives that derogatory piece about the Porthmadog sailors.

Like Emma Grayson, Gareth was moved (or ordered by a schoolmaster) to write a perception of the Gulf War. It is in the 'Modern' vogue but, I am happy to admit, that does not detract from its merit. Educationalists, these days, seem to favour blank verse, and I am beginning to lean towards the concept that one needs to be cleverer, in this medium, because one does not have the curtain of rhyme and rhythm behind which to hide.

Gareth has called his piece:-

"Airborne Warriors"

Graceful but Vulnerable;
The silhouettes are captured against a shy sun;
High above the boiling ground
The Eagles fly on.

The golden sands are empty,
Lonely, apart from the odd, solitary vehicle.
The haze, caused by the heat,
Covers the desert like a blanket.
The sun beats down on the plains below.

Scorched by the Sun, claustrophobic and scared,
Ebullient in their shells,
The Warriors wait.
Another day of the War has commenced.

* * * * * * * * * * *

It was not until we had the service, up at Treflys, to put my mother's ashes in Dad's grave, that I found out that Peggy Parmenter had been one of Mum's closest friends. Life is full of little surprises, isn't it. I have known Peggy's son, Alan, for many years. He is one 'businessman' who, in my book, deserves all the success he has achieved... and I didn't know his mum and mine were buddies.

After the service and during 'tea and cakes' back at the house, Peggy asked if I would be interested in a poem of hers. She said that it had a degree of significance to the occasion. By Crikey! How right she was!

She was worried about the use of some 'seven-lettered' words and asked if I would like to change them. I gathered, though, that the 'punch line' had been one of her husband's favourite expressions, and it seemed, therefore, sacrilegious to tamper with it.

"It's a 'B' Growing Old"

When your teeth go in a glass
And your hair starts falling out
And because you're hard of hearing
Your friends all have to shout...
It's a Bastard getting old!

When you have to wear glasses
Because you cannot see,
And cannot hold your liquor
And always want to wee...
It's a Bastard getting old!

The only consolation is
Your friends are doing it too,
Rubbing their arthritis
In sympathy with you;
Knocking back the whisky,
Keeping out the cold
And heartily agreeing,
It's a Bastard getting old!

But some of us don't make it;
Get 'cut off' in our prime;
So while we're here, enjoy it,
And have a damned good time!

* * * * * * * * * * *

I suppose the only way to approach old age is with a degree of scepticism. Until the scientists get their fingers out it is going to come to us all, eventually. Still one cannot help but admire the way these three ladies have poked fun at it.

Kath Mackenzie, by the way, is a lady I met many years ago when I first came to Porthmadog. She and her husband, Mac, God rest his soul, kept a variety of boats in the harbour and always in immaculate condition. I remember when first I was invited on board their power cruiser but was asked if I would mind taking off my boots. Of course I didn't mind! They were muddy! I had been tramping around fixing moorings. When I made it into the boat, it became even more obvious why I should have removed them. I am not kidding. You could have eaten spaghetti bolognaise out of the bilges. I have never seen such cleanliness. The engine was highly polished and not a trace of oil, salt or dust, anywhere.

I don't know which of the Mackenzies was the 'stickler'. Maybe they both had a hankering for 'Neat and Tidy'. I do know that they were both smashing people to have around.

* * * * * * * * * * *

Opposite - **Navigator**

I wonder if Kath, in her youth, was as cheeky and as single-minded as Emma Grayson who, when asked what she would like for Christmas, wrote, it seems anonymously:-

"Please Mum, I want My Ears Pierced"

Oh, come on Henrietta;
A box of chocolates,
A bag of sweets,
A new pair of roller skates?

I WANT MY EARS PIERCED!

A set of paints,
A new pencil case,
A brand new ring,
A trip to London?
Watch TV?

I WANT MY EARS PIERCED!

You can have your...
Hair permed,
Visit a Fun-Fair,
Another pet cat?
Even a new bedroom mat!
Hurry up and choose!

I WANT MY EARS PIERCED!

Play with your friends,
A box of Art straws?
Come on, Henny,
Hurry up and choose!

I WANT MY EARS PIERCED!

Come with me shopping.
How about...
An early Christmas present,
Or your own brand new dictionary?
Come on, Henny,
Hurry up and choose!

I WANT MY EARS PIERCED!

I wonder what she got... if anything!

You were promised that you would be bounced back and forth between the extremes of age and youth. What I got wrong was the number of poems about age. Well, this next one is not so much about age, as what comes after.

"Is Death the Worst Option?"

Though some may look on death with dread,
I ask, "What would you choose, instead,
Eternal life, with doubtful heart,
Bedridden , senile, ripped apart
By all those age-born hurts and ills;
Forever scoffing tons of pills?"
I think my answer would be "No!
It could be better 'down below'!
I've no complaints. I've had my time.
I've walked on air... and crawled through slime:
And when that final ending comes,
When brave St. Peter does his sums,
My 'goods' and 'bads' overtly laid
For all to see- His judgement made;
If He's forgiving, steeped in care,
I may just be allowed 'Up There'!"

* * * * * * * * * * *

Often, when I have nothing better to do, (Perhaps I should re-phrase that, in case the boss is listening). Very rarely, when I have nothing better to do, I disengage from my Earthly surroundings and try to relate my insignificance to the infinity of the Universe. I attempt, though without much success, to imagine the enormity of that nothingness, out there, which has an occasional blob of fire, scattered hither and thither, with a shell of cooler fragments, orbiting protectively around.

Isn't it mind boggling, when one remembers how far it is to walk to the corner shop. We are told that 'space' is a vacuum, which implies that there is nothing there. If there is nothing there, how can it come to an end? Even if you run out of fiery blobs and orbiting fragments, there is still the 'space' in which there is nothing. When you reach the edge of space, the border, as it were, what would be on the other side? More nothing?

Einstein had a theory, did he not, that if one went far enough into space, one came back, eventually, to the starting point, a sort of 'great circle route'! Well, if Space is, indeed circular, what, I'd like to know, lies outside its circumference?

I have a theory of my own. If you consider and accept that matter, as we know it, even dense, solid matter, consists, largely of inter-molecular space, (I am told that the ship, Queen Elizabeth, would fit into a match box if it were collapsed into its inter-molecular space,) is it not possible that the star systems, as we know them, with their orbiting planets, may simply be the atoms and molecules comprising some matter, some object, the size of which is just simply beyond our comprehension?

And what lies without that object? More space?

It is a whole lot easier to switch off, at that point.

Let's get back down to Earth. Grandson Gareth, I doubt if he knows the meaning of the word nepotism, and it is in-appropriate, any way, has written a couple of little pieces which impress me. If you remember the uncertain Winter we had, this year, and can imaging a young lad dying to do all those young-ladly things, like building a snowman, snowball fights, and so on, you may be able to sympathise with...

"That Cold White Stuff"

Snow, snow, wonderful snow;
How great it is when your nose starts to glow.
Freezing cold... wellies on..
Another day and it'll be gone!

* * * * * * * * * * *

The David mentioned below is Gareth's brother. The poem, I think, describes many a home environment in which young boys and girls are learning that most difficult human requirement- cohabitation.

"Jenna- My Temperamental Sister!"

My sister, Jenna, is only three;
She's really very cute.
But when David interferes
She causes a right dispute.

"David! Don't do that!
You naughty big boy.
Stop it! Go away!
Go and find your own toy!"

"Oh, Jenna, don't be nasty;
Mummy will give you a smack.
No! Jenna! Don't get hasty... "
One- two- three- whack!!!

She's got a good right hook;
She uses it once in a while.
But, behind that cheeky look,
Is a nice, cute smile!

I visited the family during last winter, on the one day, probably, when they did have some snow. Within a couple of hours of my arrival, the car disappeared under a drift, the electricity was off and the water frozen. Poor Jo, (daughter). With that lot to contend with, plus a visiting father and some hyped-up kids, is it any wonder that I saw, in another of Gareth's poems, an ominous reference to 'Super glue'.

"Mummy, Ive Got the 'Flu"

"Mummy, I've got the 'flu'!"
"Lie on the bed. I'll check it out!"
"Mummy, that's... not...? It is... It's g glue!"
Her problems were solved, without a doubt.
No children to pester her, no noise at long last.
Their lips would be glued until the snow passed.

There's one lad who's got his Mum weighed off!

* * * * * * * * * * *

The creation of poetry is often just one way of coping with an otherwise disturbing occurrence, practice or ideal; particularly of a controversial nature about which one cannot decide on which side of the fence to be. You know what they say about Royal Naval Officers, retired or not... They are totally unable to make decisions.

A few years ago this nation was split, somewhere near down the middle, over the question of abortion. What an opportunity to argue against one's own religious beliefs, never mind lose friends who may be of a different persuasion.

Being Fleet Air Arm, I thought 'Abort' meant 'Don't take off!' but I was quickly enlightened and joined the vast throng of undecided. Who should decide? Should it be the parents, and if so, which one? Should it be the Church, or Nature, or some joker up in Parliament?

The easy way out for a male, chauvinist pig was to ridicule the whole concept, so I wrote, and have ever since been trying to pluck up the courage to publish...

"The Anti- Abortion Lobby"

If you're anti-abortion, and all that 'stuff'
  Then Mr. Orton's Bill doesn't go far enough.
If it's wrong to kill a child in the foetal state
  There's another circumstance that I'd like to relate;
Because, when I see this 'bird' with the low cut dress
  And the shapely thighs
And the sparkling eyes,
  I'm bound to be lured by her dimpled cheeks,
If I haven't had a 'sniff' for weeks and weeks...
  So I sidle on up... and invite her to the woods
With a promise of 'The Earth' if she comes up with he goods;
  And the anticipation makes the pulse rate grow...

There ought to be a law that SHE CAN'T SAY NO!

Sorry! I know. It's very naughty.

The more advanced Mankind becomes, the more such horrible decisions will have to be taken. In spite of all the 'Science Fiction' on the subject, there are those sceptics among us who firmly believe that genetic engineering has already been mastered and practised, on a need-to-know basis, of course!

One such sceptic (I hope she will forgive me for calling her that) is Jaquie Thomson. (I hope I've spelled her name correctly, as well). Jaquie is full of deep, inner theories, explanations of the inexplicable, and so on. She even agrees with my beliefs on the structure of the Universe.

Jacqui (I've checked... that is the correct spelling) has the conviction that we humans are the result of some pretty clever genetic engineering carried out by a vastly superior culture, many thousands of years ago. They had to adapt their creations to suit the peculiar conditions of a particular planet which had a very high oxygen content in it's atmosphere and which, ultimately, came to be known as Earth.

Well, why not? There have been other explanations far less believable.

I am somewhat humbled by Jacqui's literary talents. I happen to know that she is working on a novel which will be well worth reading... if she ever will get on with it! And she has written some gripping short stories. I am honoured to be able to include an example of her 'depth' in my book.

"The Soft Voice of Unreason"

They laid my mother in a box, a padded, pure-white satin bed.
    Now, throw the flowers on to the coffin
    And hate the man who thought her nothing.
My father, crying: and in my heart a pure, blind anger bred.
    (Step softly, little William, not to wake the newly dead.)

I take in television; all its horrors, with such dread.
    A soldier kills with no good reason,
    But he'll not suffer in a prison,
A governmental sanction, and so many more have bled.
    (Tread softly, master William, don't upset your little head.)

In school, there's drugs and fighting and, each day, my fear is fed;
    As education cuts are biting
    Teachers put more stress on striking.
I fight my way through fools and mayhem, contempt of others' bred.
    (Go softly, now then William, or you're like to end up dead.)

The world I see is filled with starving people without bread;
    They're dying in their tens of thousands
    Growing war-zones on their grass-lands.
Someone grasp their outstretched hands; There's been enough tears shed.
    (Speak softly, brother William, for by God's hand are they fed.)

The dissolute, the vagrant, the lonely and the sad;
    Products of our greed and want,
    Society's lost ones; mankind's mutants,
Can we listen to their plaint, and offer them our aid?
(Break softly, Father William; to salvation are they led.)

I'll leave this world a wiser man: a futile path has led
    To my belief that no man can
    Live without faith in fellow man,
And when that faith is broken, stands alone and isolated.
And I'm damned if I'll go softly, as if I'd never been,
It's time that people realised what 'Love thy neighbour' means.
    We carry Heaven within us,
    And, likewise, carry Hell,
And what we do with our lives touches other lives as well.

I also rather like Jacqui's cynical appraisal of a beauty parlour. For someone so beautiful, naturally, it must seem quite strange that some of us have to work at it!

She has called it...

"The Milking Parlour"

Our Sam Dreams of days
 When women lie, placid, under supple, knowing fingers,
Wondering at her expertise in making them
 More in their own image
Than Nature would have had.
 Softly stroking pampered bodies,
Brown from foreign forays:
 All they seek is eternal beauty,
For forty-eight to look like twenty-two.
 They lie, and fool themselves that Sam
Has magic in her hands;
 She'll make it work for them.
And Sam looks on from behind her proper and professional facade
 At these obscene, painted, portly women of indeterminate age,
And smiles her goodbyes as she pockets her expenses.

Sort of Naughty... but Nice!

Was it a Beauty Parlour... or was it a Massage Parlour...? Or was it something else? I don't know! My memory... these days... But something, in my dim and distant past, prompted me to write my own words to a popular song of the period.

I must have been quite young and very naive. I don't know exactly when this was written but must assert that it had to be in the very late 'forties' or very early 'fifties'.

"Pale Moon"

It's not the pale moon that excites me,
The lack of a nightie-
Oh no!
It's just the nearness of you.

I had a strange non-understanding
While on the first landing
And I
Didn't know what to do.

It's not that I'm frightened by your glamour;
And neither am I put off by the fee:
It's more a kind of something in your manner
That makes me wonder what you'll do to me!

So, thank-you kindly for your offer!
The cash I'll still proffer...
But I...
I'm going to leave, if I may...
Please don't think that I'm 'Gay'!
It's just the nearness of you.

I can already hear the doubters claiming, "He must be joking! They weren't called 'Gay' in the early 'fifties'."

That may well be the case, but, we apprentices had our own slang and, as luck would have it, our word for anyone who was 'different', was 'Away'. "Oh, him! He's away, man!"... It could mean anything from 'absent' to 'as queer as a two-bob watch'; a sort of 'safe' criticism.

It is a fact that the original last-but-one line was... "Please don't think I'm 'Away'" I had to change it or no-one would have understood what I meant, would they!

Language, as a means of communication, can be dangerous!

I wonder how many people use writing as a relief valve! I know I do, and there must be lots of others... or there wouldn't be such things as 'Letters to the Editor', in our newspapers, and the average MP would not have such a vast 'Mailbag'.

Even if not aimed at a particular destination, one can often find relief in simply jotting down one's thoughts. I know that I felt much better for having written...

"A Mugging"

We're heading fast for anarchy,
   Of that there's little doubt.
The more one reads the papers,
   The more one needs to shout.
Another mugging in the town
   Last night- the fifth this week:
A lady in her dressing gown,
   An 'Old girl', frail and meek.
She only opened her front door
   To put the empties out-
The next thing, she was on the floor;
   A victim of some lout!

The place was then 'done over';
   Her purse and handbag went.
They even took the caddy in which
   She had stowed her rent.
They left her lying in the cold,
   The worst part of this crime.
It's just a miracle, I'm told,
   That she was found- in time.

I hope they catch the villains
   But it won't do any good.
The punishment they get, these days,
   Is nothing like they should.
Give that old lady freedom
   To meter out the cane
And five'll get you ten
   That they won't bother her again!

I must keep off my favourite subject. This is not a soapbox. But it does seem, these days, that more sympathy is shown to the villain than to his victim, and the very mention of the word 'discipline' can create awful tension in some circles!

It is my guess that Roberta Halling suffered her share of discipline, as a child. Now, as a young adult, she has written a poem to honour her Dad's retirement. The cynic in me detects a little bit of the 'Own-backs'.

Roberta has also given some of the members of the Careful Cowardly Comfortable Cruising Club a mention. Bob, himself, of course, is a member. Those of you who do not know about this wonderful collection of people should read Diversion Volume 1.

"Ode to Dad"

The day has come for you to retire;
Time to relax and sit by the fire;
A time for sailing, to Borth y Gest,
With Mum as look-out, up the crow's nest!
A time for barbecues, on the sun-deck,
Or a mooch round 'Ballast', in search of a wreck.
Time to master the language of Wales
While listening to more of Peter's tales.

Don't forget your treks up the street
Where John and Maureen you're sure to meet.
Ken and Gwen will be popping in
For tea, coffee, or a large gin!
Lois and Mum will be gone for hours
In search of bargains... and loads of silk flowers.

But, wherever you go
And whatever you do,
As Peter would say,
"Diollocks to you!"

I'm afraid I don't know the significance of that last line. Obviously a private joke between Roberta and her Dad. If you are consumed by curiosity, I can only suggest that you ask the lass yourself. I haven't the courage!

I am a coward! That is established fact, proven by such circumstances as when I wanted to know a friends age and hadn't the courage to come right out and ask. Instead I probed.

Was it lack of courage? Could it have been a deep seated desire to show decorum? I'd like to think so!

"How Old Are You"

A gent would never be so bold
As just to ask a friend, "How old?"
So, Harry, now your Spring has sprung,
I beg you, tell me, just how young!

Lack of courage... sense of decorum... puny arguments against the sadness of losing an opportunity for want of the ability to utter just a few, well chosen words...

Opposite - **The Ballast Island, Porthmadog**

"Faint Heart Never Won Fair Lady"

To want is not enough but to demand is too unkind:
So, all that's left is hope that you will, some day, please God, find
A small place in your heart, perhaps a corner of your mind,
As sanctuary for my soul;
And, if I plead, implore, cajole,
Would you, then, tell me what I need to know?

Or will the day come soon when longing bursts my outer shell,
My erstwhile patience gone in passionate desire to yell
Of burning love which drags me to the outer edge of Hell?
I need to find a lonely place,
A haven no-one else can trace
Where privacy allows my thoughts to flow.

To want is not enough but to demand may be too much;
Achievement in such matters may require a gentle touch.
Your smile is all I have- a fragile straw at which to clutch-
For Happiness fulfilment brings
Is nebulous as Fairy wings
And isn't the dénouement of the show!

Ah yes! Life, and the complicated business of human relationships, can be very difficult to understand.

I once read, at the invitation of my pal, Dick Forest, a passage from a book which he was reading, by James Hadley Chase.

To us, young apprentices, in the late 'forties', it had a slightly risque ring to it but, in later life, I have often thought "How true! How astute of that author to put, so concisely, such deep observations"

There is no guarantee that I have recorded the passage accurately, but the impact it had upon me must be reflected in the fact that I remember so much of it more than forty years on.

"The physical relationship between a man and a woman is so delicately balanced that the slightest, least suspected trifle may upset it. A thoughtless word or deed or even a mannerism, repeated once too often, may snuff out the flame that their association has kindled..." I forget how it goes on.

"Faint Heart", I suspect, was written by a shy, middle-aged would be lover who, sadly, had experienced the snuffing out of one flame and had realised that fulfilment of his love was not an end, nor even the beginning of an end, but maybe only the end of a beginning! Sorry, Winston!

He also discovered another sad facet of modern life, that it is impossible to admit to loving someone, male or female, without the worst possible 'slant' being attached to such an...

"Admission"

A pattern of convention has developed, to spoil the rudimentaries of life, which makes it unforgivable to care for a woman who is someone else's wife.

Society rejects the simple notion that a person may be, well, so nice to know that from quite pure and chance associations a fondness may develop, bloom... and show!

There are, however, those of us romantics, believing it to be not such a sin to entertain dear thoughts of an acquaintance and, unashamed, enjoy the warmth therein.

To love is neither noble nor irrational; it strikes with undiscriminating flare to fill the lover with a strange exuberance and, often, not an inkling of despair.

Incredibly, such love will need no favour, encouragement or sign the heart is won. Indeed, perhaps is better off not knowing for rejection would be bound to spoil the fun.

So, if you can accept that someone loves you who has no right to even dare confess, please promise not to ridicule or scorn him; he's just a harmless poet. Thanks! God bless!

Wouldn't it be lovely if there were no doubts, no dark suspicions to cloud our path through life. I know, it is all part of 'That Rich Pageant'. Without intrigue, honesty would not be worth a mention. If 'openness' were commonplace there would be no need for disbelief. How dull! I guess He knew what He was doing!

* * * * * * * * * * *

Once upon a time I worked for a Chief Petty Officer who was an 'intellectual'. He had read the complete works of T.E.Lawrence... and continually used words which I did not understand.

Not to be out-done, I sat, one night, with a dictionary and contrived to write a poem with as many 'long' words in it as I could. I think I must have been feeling a bit guilty at the time. It is as though I had made brave advances to someone who was not instantly impressed but who, ultimately, acquiesced.

I don't think my Chief was terribly impressed, either, and neither has anybody else been since... But here it is, anyway!

"Intellectual Intercourse"

Look on me, eyes of scorn, scathe me, scar and sear;
Augment my apt abasement, fire my facile fear.
Denounce my aberration, disdain my Plebeian past,
Renounce my sinful soul but, eyes, relinquish me at last.

Gaze now, uncertain eyes, so quick to sparkle hate,
Once filled with deep disgust and wont to remonstrate.
If torment be your turmoil, humility your tools,
Fill not with tinsel tears but, eyes, be acquiescent pools.

Impassioned, lucid eyes, alive with eager haste,
Desire has mulled your malice; surrender to the taste.
Grey films of satisfaction, contented, calm, benign,
Contort in ecstasy but, eyes, reflect, always, in mine!

Also while very young, but sadly not quite young enough, I spent an evening with a family in Perth, Western Australia.

It is worth a mention if only because no where else in the whole world did I experience quite such hospitality. When our ship docked in Freemantle, the Aussies were queuing up to 'Host' sailors for the duration of our visit. It really was a great gesture.

Why sad? Did I hear somebody ask? Well, I had just reached the second half of my third decade and the family who hosted me had a daughter who was an absolute peach but who was only sixteen years old!

We had a fabulous evening with lots of laughs. They made me sing for my supper... and, do you know, I was the only one there who knew all the words to "Waltzing Matilda".

Someone said, "Come and look at this!" We all collected by the open french windows and... what I scribbled on the back of 'Daily Orders', in the sanctuary of my bunk, aboard H.M.S. Albion, early the next morning, says it better than anything.

"Sunset Girl"

I stood amid a crowd, yet all alone,
Oblivious to the chatter and the drone
Of conversation held in friendly tone.
A glorious panorama filled my eyes
Of gold and scarlet, reaching o'er the skies,
Heralding the sinking of the Sun;
Blazing fanfares! Alas, day is done!

The beauty of the Heavens held me still,
And yet, served even then but to enhance
A far more stunning beauty at my side.
I knew at once, If I were e'er perchance
To dream, 'twould be of only you, Dear one,
And of the sunset that you loved - at which I cried.

And now the scene was changed. Dark, silhouetted trees
Swayed gently to and fro in evening's cooling breeze.
The gold had turned to crimson, scarlet to purple,
And all the mystery of night descended
Casting
Exotic shades upon a fragrant flower of womanhood.

Poetic charm personified, poised, perfect, beautiful!
Kind, understanding, bright, happy... wonderful!

* * * * * * * * *

Isn't it such little episodes in our lives that make us the people we are! The passions, the frustrations, the missed opportunities, for whatever reasons, shape us into bitter 'If onlies' or contented residents of our own brand of Nirvana.

I know which end of the scale I am at now. I can only guess at the various stages through which I must have travelled to arrive here; guesses rendered more 'educated' by reading the bits of poetry constructed along the way.

In 1963 I was promoted from the ranks. This required a trip to the Royal Naval College at Greenwich and brought about a purely chance re-acquaintance with my schooldays girlfriend.

This should have been the happiest period of my life. An ambition had been achieved; my dream of becoming one of Her Majesty's Lieutenants was a giant's leap closer... and yet, my emotions were torn apart.

No! I'm not blaming the schooldays girlfriend. She became a window through which I could recognise my dissatisfaction and accept the realisation that there was, perhaps, inside me, a deeper feeling towards someone than I would have cared to admit.

I remember driving my three-and-a-half litre 'Jag' at speeds far greater than was sane and thinking, philosophically, "What does it matter if I kill myself!"

There's selfish, isn't it! I might have killed some other poor soul who had good reason to live!

It was in this atmosphere that the 'sorry' little piece below was written.

"Enquiring into Life"

It is dark, yet who needs light to see?
There is death, yet who needs life, to be?
It is cold, yet who needs warmth, to love?
There is Hell, yet Heav'n is up above.

There is pain, but love brings comfort, too.
Is there truth in everything we do?
What is 'truth' if Life is one big lie
And love can only live until we die?

There is no truth in love; it causes pain.
Associations kindle, wax... and wane,
And what is left to satisfy our need?
There is desire, passion, lust and greed!

There is love... yet who needs love to live?
Enjoyment reigns- that which we have, and give!

Such feelings, such attitudes, I now deride as immature. It is easy, at my age! But, on reflection, on delving into the diary of Life, the thought occurs; "What a pity it took so long to grow up."

There is, after all, something basically wrong with the structure of civilised human beings. We mature, physically, far too early; certainly before our mental awareness has developed to a point where from it can cope with the emotional aspect of the physics.

Civilised society pushes us into what is intended to be a lifelong partnership, without practice or rehearsal, and then condemns when, sometimes, it is not 'Alright on the Night'.

At least it separates the 'Men' from the 'Boys'. The 'Men' are those who cope with their lot... The 'Boys' will always be boys!

I am going to leave you with three poems from across the spectrum. The first is by a young girl who, unwittingly, perhaps, is declaring an interest in Society and making a political statement.

Daughter Lyn showed her work to her Headmaster who, in turn, handed it to a pressman. Thus I am able to quote from the paper.

The Headline read-

"OUR HOSPITAL"

An eleven-year-old pupil at Ysgol Eifion Wyn, Porthmadog, has been so upset since she heard of plans to close the town's Madog Memorial Hospital that she composed a poem to express her feelings.

"Pulling it Down"

They're going to close our hospital which is on top of the hill;
Suppose it wasn't there when I was feeling ill!
Say I broke my leg and the hospital wasn't there;
I would have to go to Bangor in a big wheelchair.

A lot of people, I know, want the hospital to stay.
If it isn't there we can't go for an X-ray.
The Health Department moans about its empty purses;
They don't seem to care about their doctors and their nurses.

The 'Madog' has been there for ages; it is really a part of the town.
I know that I will be sad when the bulldozers pull it down."

* * * * * * * * * * *

Opposite - **The Glaslyn Horizon**13

The second is by Sister Justine who, I promised, would get a mention. She will write these enormously long poems about her Royal Marine sons. I can understand her pride but, honestly, you'd need to be Readers Digest to find publishing space.

However, before she became a Customs and Excise Officer, about which I don't wish to talk, she was a Primary School Teacher. She tells me... "My class of eight and nine-year-olds were to perform at the local Schools' Drama Festival so I elected to work on a dance, using this poem instead of music. It is written with apologies to A.A.Milne!"

I suspect it is also a slight censure of modern Society.

"Micro"

They're changing machines all over the world,
The micro-chip has been unfurled.
No more our watches do we wind,
Life has become so easy, I find, - Says Micro.

The micro-wave oven cooks Oh, so fast,
Our dinner is ready in one short blast.
Computers are here to work out our sums,
Numerical genius? It just comes, - Says Micro.

Space Invaders, all over the town,
The little creatures just jump up and down;
You can go out tonight and not miss a show!
It'll all be recorded on your Video, - Says Micro.

They're changing machines all over the world.
The micro-chip has been unfurled.
What did we do, before it came?
Our lives will never be the same, - Says Micro.

* * * * * * * * * *

The Third Poem in this winding-up trilogy is by an old misery-guts who doesn't give a damn...

Well that may not be completely true. His last verse could be claimed to represent environmental concern... or it could be that he is 'miffed' because the Quarriers have totally destroyed one of his Survey Marks.

Whatever, it is a lighthearted look at...

"The Glaslyn Horizon"

When plodding up this estuary my conscience never fails
To appreciate the magic of those glaciated dales;
Those graceful, rolling pointers which frame, but can't restrict
The majesty of the Moelwyns and the audacity of Cnict.

The Nose of Penrhyn, sticking out, is sniffing at the sea.
Just like some Giant Mongrel's snout, it cocks a snook at me:
And, hidden round the corner, fast coming on the beam,
That famous little village, the Clough Williams Ellis dream.

Abaft the starboard quarter I can see the Idris Chair;
It seems to be in favour for the sun is shining there.
On some dark, stormy night I hope I never, ever meet
The Giant whose backside once sat upon that stony seat.

Of all these elevations, the one I like the best
Should have a row of medals shining right across his chest.
He's a courageous soldier- and that's no idle boast:
He's quite the smartest Guardsman you will find along this coast.
He must be small! I climbed him- and I'm no mountaineer;
But yet he stands there, mocking, with a grin from ear to ear!
His fame has reached all corners,
To North, South, East and West.
No need for me to name him, for,
By now, you've Moel y Guessed.

If Only left to Nature, if God had placed a ban
On Human intervention, the ingratitude of Man,
That shameful scar at Minffordd would not, now, contradict
The majesty of the Moelwyns nor the audacity of Cnict.

I wish I had a pound for every time I have been asked, "Why 'Audacity'?" For an answer one only needs to look at it. (Dwell a while on page 78) Its profile, seen from the Glaslyn estuary, says, "Look at me, I'm a mountain!" when everyone knows it is only a pimple!

The Year 1992 has, for me, great importance. It contains the five hundredth anniversary of that famous voyage... Gosh, was it only five hundred years ago...

"The Bit You've All Been Waiting For"

We have, in 'Port', a Cruising Club
 Who sup their wine and scoff their grub
In Careful, Cowardly Comfort while
 The braver ones, the rank and file,
May only envy these 5 C's
 While labouring against the breeze.

In fourteen hundred and ninety two
 Columbus sailed the ocean blue;
Though what he found was quite obtuse,
 Albeit he had some excuse...
And, "What's the connection", I hear you say!
 "That happened in a bygone day!"

But he was breaking virgin ground;
 He wasn't even sure that the Earth was round!
One must accept, he did not have
 Our Radar, Decca or Sat-Nav,
But Asia he'd have found... fair play,
 If America hadn't been in the way!

I guess to some they seem remote,
 Columbus and his little boat,
When probably, and very soon,
 A man will land on a Saturn Moon.
But the Santa Maria's trip, you know,
 Took place just 5 C years ago!

So! There's the connection; 5 big C's,
 And how to navigate with ease.
One shouldn't worry if the way is lost,
 Nor place the blame, nor count the cost;
But start afresh, from There and Then!
 Put down the Sword- Take up the Pen...

AND IF YOUR READERS CRY, "SOME MORE!"

START WORKING ON "DIVERSION FOUR"

* * * * * * * * * * * * * * * * * *